Revd Mr Paxton,

with the regards of

Eli K. Price

July 1853.

MEMOIR

OF

PHILIP AND RACHEL PRICE.

"Honour thy Father and thy Mother."

PHILADELPHIA:
PRINTED FOR ELI K. PRICE AND PHILIP M. PRICE.
1852.

E. B. MEARS, STEREOTYPER.

C. SHERMAN, PRINTER.

PHILIP AND RACHEL PRICE.

Beloved and venerated parents, your memory is cherished by your children with a devoted affection: Shall they pay no outward tribute of respect, nor leave of you any memorial for the future? To you, under Providence, we owe it, that we breathe the breath of life—that we open our eyes to the glorious light—behold the beauties of all created things, and rejoice in a happy existence. To you we owe yet more; that we were trained to lives of usefulness, guided in the paths of virtue, and from your lips received the inspired words to turn the heart in love to God. With us and our children the recollection of beloved features will pass away; and shall the memory also of your worth, affections, and devoted service with us perish for ever! The thought of it brings the reproach of a delinquency in filial duty to you, and also of the neglect of the sacred obligation we owe to our posterity, to perpetuate your precepts and example, for their observance and imitation. To commemorate these I would invoke to the service more than the skill of the Egyptian art of conservation, that your character and memory might be embalmed in the hearts of our descendants in all the purity and beauty in which you lived, and yet live in the recollections of your children: And as your long lives were a bright exemplification of the power of Gospel truth, so may your memory live in its light and life, enshrined in living temples of love and devotion, for ages to come.

To commemorate by written memorial all those of good name who have lived and died would multiply books beyond the capacity of readers to peruse more than a very limited selection. The beneficence of the Creator produces in his creation the good and the beautiful in boundless profusion. The sequestered flowers that bloom unseen by human eye, and "waste their sweetness on the desert air," do not uselessly grow,—but produce a seed that in time may germinate in light, and lend a cure to the healing art. The humbly good that pass through life and challenge no admiration of men may unobtrusively instil into many hearts sentiments to be perpetuated for the moral and religious preservation of our race: And if their virtues do but bloom in the sight of the Creator's Eye, and shed a fragrance that is but an incense to Him, they will not have lived in vain.

To claim a worldly distinction for those whose endeavour it ever was—"to do justly, and to love mercy, and walk humbly with their God"—would be to act in conflict with the spirit that actuated their lives. Acting solely in obedience to their apprehension of duty to man and his Creator, such a pretension would be rebuked by the recollection of that self-watchfulness that ever guarded them against the weakness of human vanity, and accounted all that was good and excellent as emanating from a Divine Source; the merit of which man cannot rightfully claim as his own. Yet all of their history that may be useful to others, in precept or example, it is a duty to rescue from forgetfulness and loss; and to perpetuate it, is in perfect consonance with their sentiments and character. If their lives were rightfully devoted, the record of the testimony of that devotion cannot fail to be useful; and faithfully to portray, is unavoidably to commend,—for the facts speak praise: But praise cannot reach "the dull cold ear of death,"—and their offspring cannot share it but by a like deserving.

The plain and simple memoirs of Philip and Rachel Price will readily and harmoniously blend in the narrative. United early in life, they lived together in cordial affection and harmony of views for more than half a century. Born and educated in the Society of Friends, and both at an early age brought under that Divine influence which alone can constitute them truly its members, they devoted their protracted lives faithfully to the duties which its discipline, its testimonies, and its faith enjoin.

The one successively an overseer and elder and the other a minister of the Gospel, they were never called to move under diverse views, and were only separated by the calls of duty leading either to the visitation of distant places, when the sacrifice was made from the united sense of a religious obligation. These separations were felt to be privations in proportion to the intensity of their affection, but in a like degree was the sacrifice a source of consolatory reflection, when their minds were brought to the test of the inquiry whether they had fulfilled the Divine injunctions laid upon them. In the performance of the services required they were often separated in person, but in harmony of feeling, devotion to duty, love for each other and for their Maker, there was ever a unity in one mind and one spirit.

PHILIP PRICE was born the 8th day of the First month, 1764, and was the fifth in the line of lineal descent from Philip Price, who came into Pennsylvania with the Welsh settlers, who in 1682 took up Merion, Haverford, and Radnor townships, and increasing afterwards settled the townships of New-town, Goshen, and Uwchlan (1 Proud's His. 221). The name was continued to him through but a single male representative in each generation from the first settler. His father, Philip Price, of Darby, died 9 month 17th, 1811. His mother, Hannah Bonsall, of Kingsessing, was of English descent, and of a family of the first settlers in that place. They were both members of the Society of Friends in good esteem, the latter an elder, lived together in close harmony half a century, and extended to their children the guarded education recommended by the discipline of their religious society.

RACHEL PRICE, born the 18th day of 4th month, 1763, was a daughter of William Kirk, of East Nantmeal, Chester county, the tenth child of Alphonsus Kirk, who came from the North of Ireland, and settled in Centre, New Castle county, in 1689 (1 Proud, 218), and of Sibylla Davis, who was of a family of early Welsh settlers. They were also members and held in esteem in the Religious Society of Friends, and their children received from them the religious care customary in that society.

The parents of neither were wealthy, and as a grazier in Kingsessing, Philip Price in the same season suffered the loss of his stock of fat cattle by the British, and afterwards of his poor by the American army, during the revolutionary war.

William Kirk, removing from his father's residence near Wilmington, prior to the middle of last century, was a pioneer in a new settlement, and encountered the usual hardships and perils of those who first penetrate the wilderness, to fell the forest and reclaim the earth for cultivation. At an early period of this settlement, when the clearing was small and the crops in proportion, a severe winter came on, with a heavy snow three or four feet deep, and drifting, made the roads next thing to impassable. It found them destitute of provision. The father rode all day to procure a supply, but returned at night exhausted and sick, without any success. The feelings of the wife and mother were roused to make another effort to avert starvation. She set off next morning and beating her way through the snows on horseback, reached George Ashbridge's mill, now Milltown, near Westtown School, a distance of more than fourteen miles. She offered her web of homespun and next year's crop in pledge for meal; frankly confessing that they were without food and without money. The miller—honoured be his name, as yet it is in Chester county and the city of Philadelphia in the third and fourth generations—took only her word, and furnished her the meal, and offered to supply the family until the next harvest. The husband in her absence had appeased the sharpest cravings of their children's hunger by the rinsings of the kneading bowl, and at night *they* found respite in sleep. But the sleepless husband watched in deepest anxiety and sympathy for her return all the night long, during which the heroic wife had battled with the snows. She reached their cabin in the morning, with the precious store for relief, and the husband and wife, overcome with joy and gratitude, fell into each other's arms and wept,—much to the astonishment of her young brother, a lad of ten or twelve years of age, at such a manifestation of rejoicing,—who sensibly hastened to make a pot of *mush* for breakfast. This relief from the extremity of peril, our mother often told us with a like emotion, her father never could relate without shedding tears; and with tears the narrative is now written, and will often so be read by the descendants of William Kirk. It is due to truth, however, to say that the courageous woman was the first wife, Mary Buckingham, and Rachel Price was a daughter of the second wife of her father.

An amusing substitute for the mail occurred between the families. William Kirk took with him to the new settlement a dog from his father's house. It occurred that the dog got his feelings hurt and travelled off to his old home, whence, upon the like offence being taken upon a like show of disrespect, he travelled back again. Observing this infirmity of temper, or perhaps a proper self-respect and dignity, it was practised upon so as to make him the bearer of letters to and fro, inclosed in a bladder tied round his neck, so as not to be wet in swimming the Brandywine. The letter adjusted, the provocation to a departure was administered, and the excited temper sped the post dog, unconscious of the calculated purpose of which he was the victim, a distance of thirty miles, at the end of which he was welcomed by food and caresses. This incident may not be destitute of instruction to others than the canine race against suffering their infirmities to be played upon for the advantage of those more cunning than themselves.

William Kirk's eldest son, Caleb, interested for his father in his loneliness after the death of his first wife, and desirous of a good mother-in-law for the children, advised his marrying an excellent widow of the name of Coates. The father thought she was rather too old for him, and declined taking the advice, and thereupon the son courted and married her himself. The only issue of the latter marriage were three sons, one, Elisha Kirk, an eminent minister among Friends. The father, besides his ten children by his first wife, had nine by his second, the sixth of whom was Rachel Kirk. Happily, therefore, it was that the well intended advice was not taken.

Our father at earliest manhood, for deviations so slight that the world would deem them trivial and unimportant, was visited by compunctions and a repentance that produced an instant and marked effect on all his after life. Contrary to the known wishes of his parents he adopted a fashionable style of dress, and with a company of other young friends inclined to gaiety, visited first Shrewsbury and afterwards London Grove quarterly meeting. At the latter meeting, the powerful preaching of Jacob Lindley reached home to his state of feeling so strongly that he heeded not the call of his companions to rejoin them, and he returned home by himself, already experiencing the precious feelings resulting from the resolution to take up the cross and submit to the Divine will.

Thus commenced, in a ministration that made one as a

spiritual father the instrument of arresting an erring son, a friendship, that made them in after life affectionate co-labourers in the services of the Church, and in the cause of humanity.

The following fragments of correspondence indicate the exercised state of mind which followed this event,—of a youth yet considerably in his minority.

Kingsess. 23d 9 mo. 1782.

Dear Friend,—I received thy letter this afternoon, and shall endeavour to answer according to ability,—feeling much love towards thee at this time, and should have been glad to see thee at the meeting. As thee seems anxious to hear how we come on, I shall let thee know a little how it is with me in that respect. As I feel my mind much drawn from the follies and vanities of this world, which I have too much given way to, to my hurt, I find at this time that I cannot keep company with any one on the account that thee mentions. This is very much in the cross of the natural will, but I find I cannot witness true peace without yielding obedience to that forming Hand which has drawn me much from the world and worldly things, so that all prospects of entering into business or settling as thee mentions, have vanished at this time. But if way should open more clearly to enter into that business, I will let thee know, as I would as soon enter into partnership with thee as any one else. * * * I do not expect to come down to the meeting. I desire thy welfare, and that thou wouldst give up thy time more and more to serve Him for whose glory we are all created; so that when these fading things shall be no more, we shall receive an admittance into the Arms of Everlasting Peace and Rest. What will all the world be to us if we end not well at last? I believe there is no time like giving up in our youth, whilst health and strength of body are afforded us; that so we may be as lights to the world, that others seeing our good works, may glorify God, who is worthy for ever. Though I meet with discouragements sometimes, and believe myself to be as it were the hindermost of the flock, yet I feel a desire that all my companions, as well as myself, may come to see ourselves as we truly are.

I remain thy loving friend,

PHILIP PRICE.

Kingsess. the 16th of 1 mo. 1783.

MY DEAR SON,—I received thine, which was a comfort to me, and I have esteemed it a great blessing that thou art one amongst the number who are made willing to stand for the testimony of truth, and my desires are that thou mayst be more and more established, and that thou mayst not run too fast, nor loiter behind thy true guide: for what we are is by mercy and not any merit of our own. I believe it is good for us often to examine ourselves, and I can truly say that thy preservation, with that of thy brothers and sisters, is more near and dear to me, than all other earthly blessings; and that it is a great comfort to thy father and me, that thy mind has been thus early touched with that, that if strictly abided in, will lead out of great trouble and conflict in this present world, and when time here shall be no more, crown with that which neither this fading world, nor the enjoyments thereof, can ever give. And I may further say that I hope from thy example thy brothers and sisters may be willing to take up the cross. * * *

From thy mother,

HANNAH PRICE.

TO PHILIP PRICE, Jr.

Philadelphia, 2 mo. 5th, 1783.

ESTEEMED FRIEND,—Since I last saw thee at thy father's house, thou hast been the object of near care and sympathy, being confirmed in the persuasion that He whose mercy is over all His works, hath in infinite loving kindness cast the mantle of redeeming love over thee. And oh, saith my spirit, that neither heights nor depths, things present nor those that yet await thee, may ever be able to separate from this enjoyment of the love of Christ and the sweet incomes of His life-giving presence. It is only by bowing to the blessed Root and abiding in the Living Vine, that we are fitted to receive Divine instruction, bearing with patience and resignation the truly necessary preparation, even the pruning Hand. Thus is the mind enlightened, and an enlargement experienced into the mysteries of the Heavenly Kingdom, and we not only discover clearly His gracious will concerning us, but as we keep a single eye to Him, neither attempting to go forward, nor in the moments of proving and desertion, when the winter season is wisely permitted, seeking succour and nourishment short of the living eternal substance. We shall be favoured with the further discoveries of light and truth, and be enabled to withstand the unwearied enemy, however various his transformations, and mysterious his workings. That thou and I may fervently and diligently labour after this necessary and right experience, is the ardent desire of

Thy real friend,

HANNAH CATHRALL.

To PHILIP PRICE, Jr.

Kingsess. 5 mo. 1783.

DEAR FRIEND,—I have been at home about a week; since which I attended Concord quarterly meeting, greatly to my satisfaction and peace of mind. I feel a near sympathy with thee, my dear friend, under thy present trying dispensation, which I have wished might be sanctified to thy further refinement, and that we may endeavour for contentment under every allotment, which the Lord in

Infinite Wisdom is pleased to place us in. His Holy Hand is underneath His dependent children, to preserve them and lead them in paths they have not seen, and will not suffer them to be tried beyond what they can bear; but He will arise in his own good time for their deliverance. I write from a small degree of experience, being as it were left alone; but He who knows the sincerity of my heart has been pleased again to favour me at times with a glimpse of His living presence; which is a cause of humble thankfulness. In Him, therefore, let us put our trust, who is able to deliver; and unto whose Divine Protection I recommend thee, with desires for thine as well as my own establishment in the ever blessed Truth. With that love which united us in the paths of self-denial, I remain thy assured friend,

P. Price, Jr.

To —— ——.

Our mother has left her own account of her early religious impressions. "I believe children are often visited with the endearing influence of Divine Love in their hearts even in early years. When I look back to the many precious feelings that I was favoured to witness in early life, my mind is clothed with gratitude to the Author of my existence for his care of me. Often, when my pious parents were concerned to collect their numerous offspring together and read the Scriptures or some good book, the sweet impressions that I sometimes felt remain fresh in my recollection, now in advanced age. I mention this for the encouragement of parents, who may have young families coming up around them, to take up the cross and invite their children together, not merely in a formal manner, but with sincere desires for mutual improvement. Although parents may not see their pious labour and care crowned with success, yet I believe they will receive the reward of peace, and may have the hope that their concern and exercise may, like the bread cast upon the waters, be found after many days. I can freely acknowledge that the tender care of my pious parents was the means, under the guidance of best wisdom, of preserving me in my youthful days, from many of the snares into which too many of the unguarded fall, in passing along the slippery paths of youth. They were not stern or severe in their commands, but kept the way open for advice and counsel. I seldom or ever parted with my dear mother, without her saying to me something in this wise: 'Now thou wilt be from under my eyes for a short time, but remember that thou art always under the All-Seeing Eye that is watching over us in mercy.' I at that time thought there was an over anxious solicitude about me, but since I have experienced the anxiety of a mother, I feel thankful for her care."

In the 5th month, 1782, Rachel Kirk was passing by the gate of Friends' meeting-house, at Second and Market streets, Philadelphia, and was stopped by a Friend who took her hand, and asked, "Whence comest thou?" Being told the place and her name, and having answered as to the settlement in life of her sister Rebecca, whom the Friend had met before, and whom he remembered and loved, he paused and said, "Rachel, it will be thy turn next, and be careful that thou place thy affections upon virtue. Let not anything short of virtue sway thy mind. If anything inferior should gain pre-eminence in thy view, difficulties may ensue; but if virtue and piety govern thy mind in making a choice of a companion, you may walk hand in hand happily together through life, and be true helpmates to each other." Still holding her by the hand, he continued,—"Farewell: now mind what I say." This Friend was Samuel Emlen, an eminent minister, who through life seemed to have been gifted with a prophetic spirit. That casual meeting—casual so far as man can discern—in the crowded market-place, produced a lasting impression, and may have determined the current of a happy and useful life. Narrating it to her children, after she had lived in wedlock for more than half a century, and known all the experience of a long life, she said, "I thought it a remarkable interview with an entire stranger But it was of great use to me in settling my mind to make a prudent choice, which was soon after brought to a trial, having but a few days previously become acquainted with Philip Price, with whom his prediction has been verified, and as far realized as can be expected in this probationary state of trial, for our refinement and preparation for a more perfect state of existence." They were married on the 20th of the 10th month, 1784. Assisted by the opportune advice, she preferred the serious, virtuous, and solid character, to the more gay and showy, and enjoyed the felicity of a congenial companionship through life, but witnessed the moral declension of him of specious address and appearance, who had had but a momentary power to hold her choice in suspense.

Farming was the business of Philip Price. After his marriage he remained three years with his father in Kingsessing,—then four years on a farm in East Nantmeal, Chester county, when in 1791 he bought the plantation lying between West Chester and the Brandywine. At this time, like much of the surrounding country, it was in a low condition, exhausted, washed into gullies and unclothed with verdure; and partly overgrown with poverty grass, briers, and alder bushes. Writing to Judge Peters in 1796, P. Price said—"In the spring of the year 1792, I fenced off a piece of about four acres (to fold his cattle), being a part of a large field that was much reduced, washed into deep gullies in many parts, and which had been totally neglected for many years. The appearance was so disagreeable that I put no value on it when I purchased the place, though the field contained fifty acres." Mem. Pha. Ag. Soc'y. 2 vol. The highest efforts of agricultural improvement in this neighbourhood at the time of the purchase were those of a few meadows under artificial irrigation. Philip Price was in communication with Judge Peters, Dr. Mease, and others, who had begun to take a lively interest in the advancement of agriculture, and his acquaintance and observation extended to the best practical farmers and farms in the country. He commenced on his newly purchased place a course of improvement in manuring, the sowing of red clover and other grasses, and in the rotation of crops, that rapidly took effect, and rewarded his skill and labour. Lime was obtained from the "Valley," gypsum or plaster from tide water, and freely administered; the stable manure was protected by shelter, and applied without loss of strength before the autumnal seeding of wheat. Judge Peters, in publishing the communications of Philip Price and others, on the advantages of plaster of paris, says, "I have heard of none who have been more remarkably successful in the plaster system than Mr. West and Mr. Price. They have brought old worn-out lands to an astonishing degree of fertility and profit, by combining the plaster with other manures." Ib. 34.

The best rotation of crops, that resulted from experience, was to break up the sod late in the fall or early in the spring, and to plant the field with Indian corn, pumpkins, and potatoes—the former intermixed, the latter manured; the second year to sow with barley or oats, and after the removal of this crop, to plough the stubble, manure and sow with wheat in the fall, upon which was sown the clover and timothy seed, to come into use for pasture after the wheat harvest of the next summer, and to be mowed and pastured with the use of gypsum for several successive years, until the field came in rotation for a like repetition of crops. This process of careful husbandry transformed the exhausted hills of the Brandywine into their present fertile and beautiful appearance, and made them a garden spot of the world. And the worthless old worn-out "fifty acre field," its proprietor lived to see worth more than a hundred dollars an acre, in common with the residue of the plantation. To have been a pioneer in a process so beneficent and of apparently magical results, would be felt as no small honour to those who respire their happiness in the popular favour and applause. To Philip Price it was simply a source of benevolent satisfaction, in contemplating the good he had aided in accomplishing, of which his eye took a wide survey, from the porch of his mansion; but the obligation was not forgotten by his neighbours, in after years, when the members of the Chester County Agricultural Society elected him its first President.

The results of the experiments of P. Price in the use of plaster, as communicated in 1796, in answer to the queries of Judge Peters, were that on a high loamy soil it operated better than on low-lying clay ground; one to one-and-a-half bushels per acre are sufficient, repeated yearly while in clover; the effect is good with or without recent ploughing; is without liability to leave the soil exhausted, as from the effect of a stimulus, where the product is returned in manure; that it is most beneficially applied to Indian corn and red clover,—but usefully to other grasses and grain crops; and may be used advantageously with or without other manuring, and with most striking effect, if not immediately preceded by other manure. The best time to strew it is at the first harrowing of Indian corn, and on clover, with a small quantity soon after it comes up, to be repeated as soon as vegetation takes place in the spring; this giving a stimulus when most needed. The effect is most visible on a poor soil,—eight acres sowed plentifully with it without other manure, in five years became, says P. Price, "worth ten times what it was before I plastered it, the face of the soil appearing to be entirely changed, and is admired by all who have hitherto known it:" but though now (1852) in a high state of cultivation, the same article is annually used with decided advantage, on the same farm.

Early in life it became a manifested duty of Divine requisition unto Rachel Price, that she should make a public appearance in the ministry. Though it was a well settled doctrine of the Society of Friends that the gift of the Gospel ministry is not confined to either sex, yet so heavily did the weight of responsibility rest upon her mind that she diligently sought the Scriptures to find authority for exemption from the service, and consequent relief of mind. From the writings of the Apostle Paul the desired exoneration might perhaps have been gathered, if the strength of conviction and sense of obligation had been less powerful. But when she reflected that God is no respecter of persons, that His spirit is given to all, and that woman and man, are "heirs together of the grace of life," she could not doubt that she was equally under the command—"freely ye have received, freely give."

Under the solemn impressions made upon her mind when attending the funeral of an ancient friend, it was manifested to her—"now is the acceptable time;" and in a broken voice she was enabled to declare—"God is a spirit, and they that worship him aright must worship Him in spirit and in truth, for it is such that He seeketh to worship Him;" and she found in obedience the reward of peace. Again she doubted and questioned her own mission or that of any female appearing in the ministry; when Deborah Darby and Rebecca Young, English Friends, visited the meeting, and the former spoke so clearly to the subject and her condition of mind as to remove all doubting; so that late in life she was enabled to testify that—"I have never at any time since been tempted to question the propriety of women's preaching, fully believing in the declaration that male and female are one in Christ. My merciful Lawgiver and Judge, who knew that my heart was not altogether stubborn, but rather feared the putting forth my hand to the Ark unbidden, condescended to manifest His presence by breaking and handing forth a little of his Heavenly bread; and I was enabled again to taste of his goodness, and praise His Holy name as on the banks of deliverance; but with fear and trembling, lest I should add to or take away from what He should command." "Those dear Friends visited and had precious opportunity under our roof. Deborah, after saying a good deal to encourage us, particularly addressed herself to me, saying, 'Why art thou discouraged on account of the smallness of thy gift in the ministry? Doest thou not know that five words fitly spoken in season are better than five thousand without life? It is by being faithful in the little, that we have the promise of being made rulers over more.' These excellent remarks encouraged me then, and often since have afforded me instruction and strength."

In yielding to the sacrifices to be made in the discharge of her ministerial duties, she always had the support and encouragement of her husband. Both equally understood their proper relationship in respect to the conditions of this life, and in respect to obligations above all human control. In all that related to earthly affairs, free consultation and sympathetic aid subsisted, without interference with the assigned duties of the head; and also in spiritual concerns the like freedom of communion and interchange of feeling cemented their happiness, but with an implicit deference to the higher sanction of a Spiritual authorization to either. This harmonious sympathy and mutual deference imparted a moral and religious beauty to their life; and made it not only an example, but a happy illustration, as the natural fruit of the principles of their religious profession. The wife whose mind is truly impressed with the sense of religious obligation will not fail in her deference to her husband in temporal matters,—and the husband in like manner impressed could not presume to control the spiritual exercises and powers of the wife, for which, as an immortal being, she is accountable to the Almighty. Under this paramount sanction, her life of religious thought and prayerful devotion to her Creator, brings her upon a perfect equality with man, and the history of the Society of Friends has been adorned with many instances in which woman has excelled in the powers of persuasive conviction and true religious eloquence. Apart from the gifts of natural talent and spiritual endowment, she ever addresses hearers prone to believe in her superior purity of life and thought, her greater sincerity of belief, warmth of affection, and more ardent devotional piety. This condition of the hearer is the best commencement to persuasion—and under it the guarded, perhaps hardened heart, admits more readily the divine visitation that leads to condemnation, repentance, and submission.

An early lesson of instruction to our mother, which remained with her through life, and is left for her children, was derived in this wise: She had heard John Simpson very instructively in the ministry, and particularly so in explaining the mysteries of the Revelations; and on an expected visit from him, looked forward to it as an occasion of spiritual instruction in respect to the sublime truths, which had so interestingly engaged his mind in the ministry. She was disappointed to find him drawn to speak familiarly of his farming operations, and to abstain from those high and serious matters her own mind was dwelling upon: and among other things he narrated was the occurrence of a disorderly contest among his hands in the harvest field, whereby they injured his wheat. He started to arrest their proceedings, determined to turn some of them out of the field in a hurry, but was himself arrested in the way by a voice which inwardly spoke to him in the language, "John, govern thyself before thou art rightly qualified to govern others." He sat down until his own mind was quieted, then went to the men, addressed them upon the impropriety and ingratitude of wasting the grain bountifully bestowed for our sustenance by a merciful Creator; and was heard with respect and submission, all steadily resuming their work. Our mother concluded this to be the lesson she most stood in need of as one of the heads of a large family of various dispositions, saying, "I felt the necessity of keeping self under proper control in order for the right regulation of those about me; and the incident was often recurred to in silence for my own improvement, and sometimes recommended to others for their advantage."

One of the earliest occasions of prolonged absence of either from home on a religious journey, apparent from their correspondence, was the accompaniment by Philip Price of Charity Cook, and Susanna Hollingsworth, of South Carolina, on a visit to the meetings of the Society in Virginia and Western Pennsylvania, during the severe winter of 1796–97. The crossing of the mountains was then a difficult task, not free from danger. He writes from Virginia: "I wish thee may be favoured to bear with patience my absence, being in hopes it is still right for me to go on with them, however trying it may be. I feel an earnest desire of being found in my allotment (of duty). I have had some heavy exercises to pass through since I have been from home, both on my own account and on that of the Society, but I have endeavoured to come into a state of resignation, wherein I now enjoy a good degree of peace of mind. * * I could write a good deal more, but must decline at present, as it is so cold the ink freezes in my pen, although near a good fire." From Redstone he wrote, "Way has been wonderfully made for us to get along, without meeting with any accident or injury, yet not without great dangers, wherein we have experienced that Preserving Power to be near in our greatest straits, who I have no doubt has called for the present dedication. My faith has never been more closely tried, I believe, on any occasion." * * * "I have no doubt but thou feels thy situation lonesome and often trying in my absence, but I have a hope thou art preserved in patience and submission to the Will of Him to whom we ought to submit in all things, and let these trials work for our further refinement and purification." * * "I often remember my dear children, and have no doubt of thy care over them, which makes me feel easy on their account. Oh that they may be preserved in innocency and virtue, which I hope will be more our concern for them than anything besides in this fading world." On their return journey he again writes, "the labour of my dear devoted companions has been close and searching in most places where our lot has been cast, but they have been enabled to discharge their duty so as to pass along with much peace of mind, of which I am sometimes favoured to partake a share in feeling a silent travail for Zion's prosperity. There appear to be many in most places who depend upon the labours of the faithful traveller, and neglect the work in themselves, which makes me fear the things which belong to their peace will be hid from them. It has been a baptising time to the churches in many places, but mournful to behold the little fruit that is brought forth to the praise of the Great Husbandman, who has so freely sent forth His labourers. I often feel my mind deeply impressed in beholding the low state of things amongst us, and under discouragement when I behold how many things are suffered to eclipse the beauty that would shine more and more from amongst us, were we to live up to what we are called, and what we profess to believe." * * "I often wish for thy dear company in these closely trying seasons, which I have often met with, thou knowest, when we were together, and have been increasingly my lot since we parted. But when I come to a state of resignation I am favoured for a time to feel a degree of peace, which is what I have longed to experience more than any other enjoyment in this world, and it is to be preferred to everything besides." The responses of his beloved wife breathed the same deep religious dedication and sympathizing affection. "My anxiety for thy preservation is at times past description, though at some times I am favoured with resignation and patience to bear thy long absence from me with more fortitude than I expected. I feel my mind measurably supported under it at this time, yet often, very often, forcibly feel the want of thy tender, sympathizing, and endearing company, in my present trying situation."

A lasting friendship was formed between these travellers, who had moved together in that "unity of spirit which is the bond of peace." A correspondence ensued after Charity's return, and while on a visit to Europe, in the affectionate terms of a mother to a son, by which title she addressed him.

In the fall of 1798, the yellow fever prevailed with great fatality in the city of Philadelphia. In their humane efforts to relieve the sick and dying, Philip's brother Isaac Price (a member of the Board of Health), was prostrated with the disease, and his brother-in-law, Edward Garrigues, exposed to imminent danger in attending the sick. These were both remarkable men. Isaac was of a happy and joyous temperament, and his gayety a degree beyond what his more sober brethren could fully sympathize with; but not less innocent, humane, and devoted to the high calls of duty, to which at this period his life fell a sacrifice. Edward, of a French descent, possessed extraordinary physical energy, courage, and force of character, to young, superficial observers, apparently uncongenial to the mild and subdued character of the Friend. Yet he bowed with implicit submission to the power of religion, owned its gentle influences on the heart, and was ever ready to serve with alacrity and zeal the cause of truth and humanity, and to extend hospitality and aid in the progress of those travelling in the ministry and service of the Church. Responding 9 mo. 10, to a letter from Philip Price, "truly consoling" and acknowledging a "tender sympathy," he writes, "Our brother Isaac is in a quiet, composed frame * * his mind evidently striving for best support;" and on the 15th, "Our dear Isaac is considerably better in health, and I hope is likely to be raised up once more as a monument of Divine mercy, and that he with many more may not only be willing to sing His praise, as on the banks of deliverance, but also remember His marvellous works." * * "I hope your benevolent minds, who have been engaged for the accommodation of the distressed citizens of this once highly favoured city, may enjoy in this lot the hundred fold of peace, and joy unmixed in a never ending eternity." The improvement that gave hope in the morning was but the prelude of the approaching dissolution that took place on the evening of the same day, as announced in a subsequent letter. "It hath pleased the Almighty Father of Mercies to release the spirit of our dear Isaac this evening. He was favoured with much composure, and an easy passage, I trust to everlasting rest." Next morning at 7 o'clock, he adds, "I have just returned from attending the last office to our brother. * * Dear Stephen Grellet, the sure friend of distress, and most excellent nurse, not only attending our brother with the assiduity of a near connexion, but at this early hour I found he was most willing to accompany me to the grave. His company in my family I hope and trust will add a blessing by his exemplary deportment." On the 29th he further writes, "It has pleased the great *I Am* to mitigate this dreadful pestilence, which has hurried more than three thousand souls into a boundless eternity." * * "The sweet solacing comfort in some of the chambers where I have attended has never been exceeded, at any former period of my life. Oh, that I may, with many, very many more, improve under the awful dispensation!" Again, a month later, he says, "Oh, that the sufferings of the present day may soften my hard heart, so as to make a lasting impression, and not be as the morning cloud which soon passeth away."

An anecdote illustrative of the fearless character of Edward Garrigues is in traditional remembrance in the family, which may be more easily excused by Friends as occurring while he was yet a young man. An American officer during the revolution, in the entry of Cook's building at Third and High streets, undertook to abuse the Quakers in general and his father-in-law Philip Price in particular, as Tories, for which Edward took him to task, and reminded him how often Philip Price had fed him and the American soldiers with tubs of soup in his orchard at the Swedes' Church, Kingsessing. The officer's temper got roused as he was worsted in the argument, and he drew his sword on Edward, who instantly wrested it from his grasp, and seizing the officer by the waistband, pitched him over the lower half-door then in use, sprawling into the street, much to the amusement of the soldiers who witnessed the feat. It is not related whether this circumstance led the officer into serious reflection and amendment of conduct, but certain it was that he afterwards reformed, became convinced of Friends' principles, and an eminent minister in the Society.

The loss by death of one brother and the failure in business soon afterwards of the other, increased the care and anxiety of Philip Price, junior, as the next friend and protector of their families; and he discharged his duty as such towards them, and to others later in life having like claims, faithfully, affectionately, and liberally, and transmitted as an inheritance the like duty and obligation to that daughter who had lived with him and most immediately represented him in position, as she also did in disposition, and a kind and considerate care and concern for all who had claims as relatives and friends.

In the years 1800 and 1801, John Hall, an English minister, was a frequent inmate in the family of P. and R. Price, and his cheerful temper and pleasant humour made his company as acceptable to the children, as were his religious experience and instructive conversation grateful to their parents. At considerable sacrifice in leaving a young and numerous family, P. Price accompanied him in his visits to the meetings of Friends in the eastern part of Pennsylvania, as far as Muncy, Catawissa, &c., into the State of Delaware, and part of New Jersey. These occasions of absence are spoken of as seasons of trial, but in the end rewarded with the feeling of peace resulting from the discharge of apprehended duty. He writes, "I do not know that I ever left home with my mind under more embarrassments, but have since been favoured to get into a more quiet and resigned state of mind, and I believe I never experienced a time wherein I felt a greater necessity of putting my trust in that Power which is able to carry us through every trying dispensation we may meet with." "Dear John has been much favoured, being more enlarged than I have known him at any time before. The number of Friends (in Delaware) is generally small at each meeting, but many other people often attend, to whom the call seems much to be extended." From New York, 4 mo. 15, 1802, John Hall wrote, "I expect by this time thou hast heard of my coming to this place under a prospect of embarking for my native land, and can now inform thee, that through an humble attention to the pointings of the Great Shepherd of Israel, I have been favoured to see the right time to leave this country, I think in as clear a point of view as I did to come here, which I esteem a great favour, among many others I have been made a partaker of. Though my trials have been many, and in depths often, yet I have no cause to complain, but in humility of heart set up my Ebenezer, and say, Hitherto the Lord hath helped me. It felt solemn to my mind in parting with thee and thy beloved wife, to whom I have felt my mind nearly united in the near bonds of gospel fellowship, and though we are parted one from another, yet are often present in spirit and in epistles written on the fleshly tablets of the heart, by the blessed Head of the Church. As He and His Father are one, even so we are one in the Covenant of Life, being made partakers of the same spiritual bread. My leaving the city (of Philadelphia) was a solemn time to me, and I rejoiced in being favoured with so many united and concurring testimonies from my dear friends in that place, that I left them in the right time; and their prayers for my preservation were as marrow to my bones. There is a precious remnant in your parts to whom I feel my mind nearly united: May the Lord preserve them as in the hollow of His holy hand."

In the retrospect of his American travels and service, John Hall wrote from "Broughton, 11 mo. 16, 1803—Beloved friend (Philip Price)—Although about eighteen months have passed over since I conversed with thee through the medium of my pen, yet I can assure thee that my love and affectionate regard for thee, thy dear Rachel, and beloved children, is not the least abated or worn out; for I can tell thee that by my fireside, and when in my bed, my mind frequently takes its flight over the great Atlantic Ocean, to visit many of my dear Friends; and thy habitation often has a large share. I often call to mind the many pleasant days and nights I spent with you and your beloved children. It was truly a place of rest to the sole of my foot, because I found the Sun of Peace to be there. May you, my dear friends, be so far preserved as still to be in the abodes of peace. This will make amends for all. I believe you have your trials and exercises as well as others for the Truth's sake, and happy are they who continue with the Master in his afflictions. I believe the same promise that was formerly made to his disciples will be your reward—'Ye are they who have continued with me in my tribulations, and I appoint unto you a kingdom.'" * * *

Towards the close of the last century, the Yearly Meeting of the Society of Friends, held in Philadelphia, had come to the resolution of establishing a Boarding School at West-Town, for the better and guarded education of the youth of the Society. In the year 1795, Philip Price was appointed one of the committee, which had charge of the construction, opening, and supervision of the institution. In this capacity he continued to devote much of his time from his first appointment until the year 1818, when Philip and Rachel Price were appointed the Superintendents, in which offices they remained until 1830, making a connected service of thirty-five years for the welfare of that School. There were educated successively all their ten children, commencing with the day of its opening in 1799; and to it those children owed nearly all that they received of an education beyond the primary instruction of the country schools. The course of studies did not then extend to the languages, but it was so much more and better than that then prevalent in the country as to be an invaluable blessing to them, and to the large numbers who have been educated there, numbering generally about two hundred of both sexes at a time, through now over half a century. The value of the instruction derived at this seminary has been of incalculable service to the members of the Society of Friends, putting them generally in advance of others in otherwise equal circumstances, for intelligence, respectability of character, and power of usefulness. And though the immediate benefit be exclusively to members of the Society, the remote advantages have been widely diffusive through many of the States of the Union, not only from the number of educated citizens sent forth to mix as active members of the community, but by multiplying good teachers to spread largely the benefits of education. How much the Society of Friends have thus been the benefactors of the country it would be difficult to over-estimate, and it is a stream of beneficence that flows in perpetuity.

It was during the superintendence of Philip and Rachel Price, that some of the local improvements of the property were commenced, that have been since greatly advanced in the laying out of walks and planting of trees, now become groves of ample size, for shade and scenery; in keeping with the beautiful and varied landscapes that surround this quiet retreat of learning. But it was the moral and religious government of the household, composed of teachers, caretakers, assistants, and pupils, in which their usefulness was chiefly conspicuous. It was in consonance with the views of the Society and with their own characters—mild, considerate, and parental. All found there the best comfort and solace in their separation from parents and home—affectionate and sympathizing protectors and friends; and departing thence, they carried with them into the world an affectionate remembrance to be retained through life. It thus occurred, from this long superintendence of West-Town, and afterwards of their own school at West Chester, that few persons have become the object of affectionate attachment and personal regard to so many individuals.

In the 7th month, 1801, Rachel Price joined Sarah Newlin in a visit to the meetings and families of Friends in the Southern Quarter, in Delaware and the Eastern Shore of Maryland. Discouragement attended her outset. "My mind was very much tried and borne down with the prospect of being so long separated from thee and our dear children, and remained so until I came to Duck Creek Meeting, where I felt almost ready to shrink and turn about homewards, when this language was lovingly presented to my mind—'Thy Maker shall be thy husband'—which proved a real consolation to my poor lost mind. Oh, may it be my greatest concern to endeavour to keep low, and experience my own will brought into subjection, and thereby experience His divine presence to be near, for verily without Him we can do nothing as we ought to do, and mayest thou find Him to be thy support and stay in my absence, and may His holy arm be round about and preserve our tender offspring from harm." And of later date, "The thought of being detained so long from home seemed almost more than my nature could bear, * * yet I believe that there is no cause of dismay, as the service seems to be owned by the Master." "My dear children, you may be ready to conclude that my love for you is not very great, or I could not leave you so long: but let me tell you that I never felt the tender ties of nature more forcibly, than since my absence from you. How often has my mind been raised in secret supplication to the Father and Fountain of all our blessings, that He may be pleased to preserve you as in the hollow of his Divine hand; yea, oftener than the returning morning." And again—"Although I feel very much tried at times on account of my being so long separated from my endeared connexions, whom I feel increasingly dear to me in my absence, yet am I favoured to experience my mind so strengthened and supported through the various dispensations I have had to pass through, as to induce me to believe that I am in my place in thus giving up. Although we feel ourselves poor weak things, to be thus engaged and often have to go down unto suffering, as I believe, with the seed, which lies low and oppressed in many minds, yet we find a little remnant in every place, which our hearts can unite with and encourage. Although weakness is often our portion, yet blessed be that Holy Arm of Power which we have found to be near for our help in the needful time of trial."

She received in response from her husband this encouragement:—"Although thy company thee knows would be very desirable at home, I hope thou wilt be favoured to be easy about us until thy mind is at full liberty to return with peace. I have been so far much preserved in the patience, beyond what I expected, and I hope I shall be favoured so to continue until the right time for thee to return." * * "Let us be content to drink the cup that is allotted us, if we are persuaded it is the Will of the Great Master, however trying, as the alone way to peace of mind. I hope thou art faithfully given up to do thy part of the work, not looking too much at thy own littleness, remembering that from those that had not great offerings to make, a turtle dove or young pigeons were accepted." Similar encouragement is repeated in later letters. "Having set thy hand to the work it will not do to look back, otherwise thou wilt lose the reward which I believe those are favoured to experience who are faithfully given up to do in true sincerity of heart. The work in which you are engaged, I have no doubt, is great and arduous, and thou art often looking to thy own weakness and inability, but I trust that He that has required this at your hands will preserve and carry you through every trial and discouraging prospect. * * Then, I trust, thy peace will flow as a river, and His living presence be felt to dispel the gloomy clouds which have often gathered and been ready to break over thy head, and overwhelm as in the deep." Further letters acknowledged the kindness of Friends visited, and that the service of the travellers "was all to pretty good satisfaction," "strength being mercifully given to relieve their minds."

Sarah Newlin returned home apparently well, but with the seeds of disease in her system, as on the day after her arrival she was attacked with bilious fever. Our parents hastened to her, found her in a sweet and submissive state of mind: she declared her work was done, and after severe bodily suffering, within a week of her return, her life fell a sacrifice to her devotion in the service of her Creator.

It was about the year 1792, that Rachel Price first appeared in the ministry. After a period of probation her service was approved; and some notes left by her manifest the feelings that accompanied the event. "My friends of the Monthly Meeting of Concord thought it right to acknowledge and recommend me to the Quarterly Meeting of Ministers and Elders, as an approved minister. A minute to that effect was furnished the Select Quarterly Meeting, in the 4th month, 1802. I attended that meeting in the 5th month, when the language of encouragement was handed forth by our valuable friend Eli Yarnall, in his usually impressive and affectionate manner. I considered it a privilege to be permitted to sit with those to whom I felt so nearly united, and to become associated with and placed more particularly under their care: but I found my exercise and concern not diminished thereby, nor my ability increased,—neither were my besetments lessened, by becoming incorporated with such valuable companions. After attending several meetings of the kind, and feeling rather disappointed, as I supposed if all were as good as I thought we ought to be before we were admitted to the Select Meeting, we might expect these to be Heavenly Communions without earthly interruptions,—and querying in my own mind why these meetings were sometimes so lifeless, even more so than the large mixed assemblies, Samuel Smith, of Philadelphia, arose and spoke very interestingly. He said,—'We are informed in the Book of Job, that when the sons of God came to present themselves before the Lord, Satan came also among them; and he believed there was not a station or situation that a man can attain unto in this life, beyond the assaults of the enemy of our souls' salvation; hence the necessity of the sacred injunction to all to watch and pray lest ye enter into temptation: that it is no sin to be tempted, but it is by obedience to temptation that we commit sin.' He apprehended there might be present individuals who had not been long admitted to that meeting, and might have expected there would be but little to interrupt the worship in spirit and in truth. He thought it was in the ordering of Best Wisdom, if it was often permitted to be otherwise, that we might feel our own weakness and dependence; that of ourselves we can do nothing to advance the cause of righteousness on the earth; that no flesh might glory in its own perfection, but that we might lie low in the abasement of self, so that He, whose right it is to rule and reign in our hearts, may direct according to his pleasure. If we who compose this part of the Society, were permitted generally to partake of the effusions of Divine love and regard, we might be induced to think that we had attained a higher state of perfection than our fellow members, and thereby become exalted in our own imaginations, ascribing that to the creature which only and alone belongeth to the Creator. This communication was very instructive and interesting to my inexperienced mind at the time, and strengthening when recurred to since. The substance yet remains fresh upon my memory (at the age of seventy), and I am willing to put it upon record and leave it, hoping that it may afford some comfort to some tried and discouraged minds when I am gone."

For some weeks in 1802, Philip Price travelled with Richard Mott, of New York, visiting the meetings of

Friends in the south-eastern counties of Pennsylvania. The services of this ministering Friend are described as having been very close upon the unfaithful, in instances producing deep contrition, but unproductive of full relief to the mind of the faithful labourer, who apprehended he had passed by some meetings that he should have taken in his course. During this and other absences of her husband, Rachel Price directed the business of the household and farm with judgment, and was concerned to attend the meetings with the children, taking with her "seven or eight of them," a distance of two miles to Birmingham.

During the spring of 1804, Sarah Talbot and Rachel Price made a religious visit among Friends in Middle and East New Jersey. Leaving Philadelphia under discouragement, the latter wrote, "With health not very good, yet my mind enjoys such a comfortable degree of quietude in the belief that I am in the way of my duty, that I have scarce language to describe the different feelings of my mind now." * * "We are permitted sometimes to partake as it were of a brook by the way-side, whereby we are encouraged to move forward in the ability received, to the relief of our own minds." In the spring of 1805, they continued their travels together among Friends of South or West New Jersey: At Salem, met with John Simpson, Thomas Scattergood, "and many other precious Friends. I felt myself a poor thing amongst them, as thou mayest suppose, yet am favoured at times from a degree of experience to acknowledge that in *His* presence there is life, and at His right hand there are rivers of pleasure forevermore." "We have been at meeting every day but one since we left home. Surely, some may say, we might be very good by this time, if going to meeting would make us so; but if we are but made sensible from time to time, that we are in the way of Divine appointment, and suffered to partake of even the fragments of the true bread, after witnessing it to be broken amongst us, so that we may know that we do indeed live, I believe we shall be satisfied." At Egg-Harbour, R. Price probably first saw the ocean, with the lively sensibility and reverential emotion with which the great works of the Creator ever impressed her sensitive mind. "I am seated at the window, delighted with beholding the waves of the sea continually rolling, wave after wave, and breaking on the shore. Oh, how awfully majestic,—how great the power, that hath set bounds even to the sea, and said 'thus far shalt thou go and no farther: There shall thy proud waves be stayed.' He hath placed the sand for the bound of the sea, by a perpetual decree, that it cannot pass it; and though the waves thereof toss themselves, yet can they not prevail; though they roar, yet can they not pass over it."

The journey was pursued to satisfaction, but under circumstances of trial and discouragement to the partner left at home. She writes, "I have found my mind very much resigned to my present allotment, whether in heights or in depths, so that I am but made sensible that I am in my place, and through Divine favour I may say (I trust without boasting) that I have from time to time felt the reward of sweet peace, which is all I crave for myself, hoping that thou wilt be made a partaker of a large share in thus giving me up." He, under the besetting trials, exclaims,—"Oh! patience and resignation to Divine allotments, how much do I still want of their influence to bring all into subjection, and be able to say, 'not my will, but Thine be done in all things!' and to bear crosses and adversity with the same calmness and fortitude as if all prospered, and was to our outward desires. Perhaps it is best for me to feel the hand of adversity and disappointment, lest I should grow forgetful and lose the sense of a grateful mind for the favours that are enjoyed." And again,—"I believe I have felt thee to be as near and precious to my life as at any time of it; indeed, our separation, I think, has felt more trying. I have been almost afraid to put my pen to paper to communicate with thee, lest I might imprudently drop something that might do more harm than hearing from us would give comfort, as it has not been my allotment to be much refreshed with the stream of consolation since thy absence: but enough, lest I now commit the error I have been afraid of."

An interval occurs in the preserved correspondence until the year 1807, when the next journey in a religious service, was undertaken. The recollections of the writer, though then young, extend back to this period. He was then and for some years after, in conformity with the practice of making all the children actively useful, assisting in the business of the farm. Though frequently taken from home by the calls of the Society of Friends, meeting the School Committee, &c., yet upon all urgent occasions, and in matters requiring skill and judgment, Philip Price was an important workman on his plantation. With his own hand he sowed the grain, the grass seeds, and plaster,—struck the furrow for planting and drilling; ploughed and harrowed the corn; and pitched the hay and grain sheaves at harvest, with an elasticity of muscle and endurance of fatigue that few could equal. He was a practical farmer, of efficient energy, and sound judgment, skilled in the choice and management of stock; and an experienced grazier lately told the writer that he had received from him his first and best lessons in the selection of cattle. He had a capacity to make riches, but he preferred to educate his numerous family; to fulfil the higher duties he believed he owed to his Creator; and to keep the tempting cares and ambition of the world beneath his feet.

It was about this period, that P. Price, with one of his daughters, made a journey into Virginia, to procure the seed of the Virginia thorn. These were the commencement of the beautiful thorn hedges that have since so much prevailed on and in the neighbourhood of his farms, dividing the rolling country of the Brandywine hills into fields of luxuriant grass or waving grain, which when ripening for the harvest, make a striking contrast with the green and neatly trimmed borders. The view of this scene from Osborn's hill, or similar elevations, can never fail to inspire a sentiment of love for our commonwealth, its happy and prosperous people,—and of gratitude to the bountiful Creator, who has spread plenty over the land and clothed it in surpassing beauty.

In order to keep the farm free from weeds, it was a constant practice of Philip Price, to pull up the docks, mulleins, cockle, thistles, &c., by the roots, before the seed ripened for a new growth; and it was a rule with him not to pass by such a weed without eradicating it, whereby the task was lessened each year, and the plantation freed from such mischievous intrusion; and for a like reason the parental care of both father and mother, was constantly watchful to eradicate all noxious weeds as they appeared to take growth in the minds of their children, before they got firm root, or went to seed for a new crop, and to sow good seed in their stead, and nourish the growth of good plants, to keep under those of a deleterious nature, and by the like continued watchfulness and care the task came to be less needed on the part of the religiously concerned parents.

The household arrangements were upon the footing of a republican simplicity. The best of plain food was provided for all, and ordinarily all, employers and employed, sat down to the same table: nor was there any loss of respect sustained by this equality of treatment; but on the contrary, a salutary influence, and parental constraint, conducive to discipline and order, not repulsive to innocent cheerfulness, were accompanied by a feeling and confidence that the welfare of all was cared for and protected.

No spirituous liquor was used on the farm, though the practice prevailed among others than Friends. In the cause of temperance, peace principles, and anti-slavery, the Friends had effectually done their work, wisely and prudently, generations before the modern zeal displayed upon these subjects; and all true Friends then, before, and ever since, have availed themselves of all suitable opportunities to advance their humane testimonies on these subjects, upon those in authority and among the people. Their progress was steady—carried forward by the process of persuasion and conviction—and sustained by the power of consistent example. It, therefore, knew no relapse or reaction, as occurs when partisan zeal becomes cooled, and excitement subsides. Their testimonies upon these subjects of human reform, Friends are bound by their Discipline to ever uphold and maintain, and so long as they shall remain true Friends, must they carry on the good works, faithfully, consistently, and steadily, not only to preserve themselves free from taint and infirmity, but to be the perpetual warners and reformers of mankind. May they ever persevere in their good and glorious mission in the way that they have so long persevered, having made their lesson effective by beginning at home, and then presenting their example to enforce their reasonings and persuasions. It is true this practice may not produce sudden demonstrations of success, but it more than compensates by its mildness, constancy, and endurance, and it is the course most consistent with the character of Friends, because in their conduct and teaching they are ever bound to exercise that wisdom which is peaceful and long-suffering, temperate, kind, and charitable. The first example to mankind of admonition and judgment, was not hasty or violent, but the voice of the Lord was heard as he walked "in the garden in the cool of the day"—and it was without any sharp accusation, woundingly to produce rebellious recoil.

Among the reminiscences of the plantation, is the fact of the frequent visits and sojourns there of coloured people, in fear and distress, fleeing in pursuit of liberty. They ever found there shelter, sympathy and aid, those claims of humanity which, though it might be penal to recognise, no true Friends could deny. Slavery, originating in the captivity of war, fraud, or oppression, could in their view gain no valid sanction by lapse of time or the authority of human law, when thus based on error and injustice. Yet neither by sentiment nor deed would they countenance any act to weaken the general authority of established government, on which the security of so many invaluable rights of person, property, and reputation depend. Wm. Penn recognised it as a great end of government "to support power in reverence with the people, and to secure the people from the abuse of power." Our civil institutions are habitually recognised by the Society as excellent, and deserving their respect and obedience, and where they cannot conscientiously acquiesce in the requisitions of laws that conflict with their testimonies, they patiently submit to the penalty, thus bearing a willing testimony to principle through sacrifice, in the hope that the world may be awakened to see and correct all errors that lead to wrong and oppression. They are the peaceful champions of the world's reform, believing that as truth and righteousness are mighty, they will, as the world becomes enlightened, prevail. No people so peaceful and conservative can fail to value highly the constitution that secures the Union of the States, and thereby preserves the domestic tranquillity and the peace with foreign powers; a constitution in which all the citizens find their safest anchorage for all vested rights and title to property, in the prohibition of all state laws that can impair the obligation of contracts. It tolerates, it is true, an evil it could not consistently name, but it was the best that could, under the circumstances, be formed. Its framers were under a compulsion so to form it as to obtain the consent of independent slave-holding states, or to abandon the task. The alternatives were disunion, and border wars, insecurity, weakness, and the final extinction of republican freedom; and Union, with peace, prosperity, strength, and the perpetuity of the great example of free institutions, and man's power of self-government, on the basis of the greatest good of the greatest number.

The uncompromising hostility of Friends to slavery, is not factious, violent, or abusive; but, proceeding from a deep religious and moral conviction of its injustice and impolicy, their opposition is based upon an established testimony, from the support of which they cannot swerve so long as Quakerism shall endure. It is a hostility that is patient, resolute, and candid, and speaking in behalf of humanity, it is only fearful of doing aught to mar the progress of a good work. Pacific in principle, they can excite to no violence; Christian in practice, the sword must be sheathed; and as the fetters are imposed by masters who only can repeal the law, that authorize their infliction, the appeal must be made to the public opinion of the states which tolerate slavery. That opinion cannot be favourably reached by abuse and denunciation, or by any method that will arouse the passions, disturb the reason, and array the feelings in hostile reaction. The legislator, exercising the prerogative of sovereignty, must be reasoned with, to convince his reason, and his passions tranquillized, that he may listen to the voice of humanity within his own breast. Nearly a hundred years ago, John Woolman, in his tenderly conscientious and beautiful writings—[often, and on his death-bed, recommended by Philip Price to the perusal of his children] afforded the best example of effective writing upon this subject; and he published in the midst of slaveholders without offence, because he calmly addressed that reason and humanity, the possession of which no civilized men dare to disclaim. Friends have, accordingly, at all times kept the door open for friendly entreaty and the convincement of the masters; have securely performed religious visits to the South, and held meetings with the slaves for religious worship; but no clandestine conduct hostile to legal claims was ever practised there by members of good repute in the Society. To the slaves they preached the patient and peaceful religion of the Gospel; to the masters the obligation of kindness and mercy, and the duty of doing unto others as they would have others to do unto themselves. But it would be to expect quite too much to believe that any true Friends should in any manner aid in the restoration of fugitive slaves, or that they would not afford them comfort and facility in their flight.

Regarding them as fellow beings and co-heirs of immortality, they admit the obligation towards them to do unto them as under like circumstances they would be done unto, and thus yield obedience at the same time to the Christian and Mosaic Law, the latter declaring that—"thou shalt not deliver unto his master the servant which has escaped from his master unto thee." But if the master come and take his servant, they can offer no resistance.

The example and influence of Friends, aided by the co-operation of a Bryan, Reed, Franklin, Morris, Rush, Peters, Rawle, and other philanthropists, led to the abolition of slavery in Pennsylvania, and the subsequent protection of those unlawfully held in bondage. It was in the midst of the American revolution that the people became awakened to a sympathy for others' woes by their own sufferings, and on the 1st of March, 1780, was passed a statute the most just, and the preamble the most responsive to the voice of humanity, of any before placed on the statute book of any nation. Reciting their grateful sense of the aid of the Divine Being in the national struggle for liberty, the patriots of the revolution conceived it to be their duty, and rejoiced that it was in their power, "to extend a portion of that freedom to others, which had been extended to them;" and feeling their "hearts enlarged with kindness and benevolence towards men of all conditions and nations"—enacted that slaves should be for ever released

5*

from thraldom in the State of Pennsylvania. It was a peaceful, patient, earnest, yet wise perseverance that led to so happy a result, and placed upon the statute book its most luminous pages. May the same wise counsels, pacific and humane spirit, ever continue to plead the cause of the oppressed, and lead to further triumphs of humanity, —pacific, bloodless, and glorious!

In the 6th month, 1807, Mary Witchel, a friend from Bradford, England, and Rachel Price, started on a religious visit to Friends in Ohio and Virginia. No turnpike had then been made across the Allegheny Mountains, and the narrow and steep wagon track, in soft places, was cut into deep ruts, and in others was rough and stony. The women Friends in crossing the mountains were obliged to dismount from the carriage and walk, or ride alternately the single riding-horse, on a man's saddle, going at the rate of two miles an hour. Rachel Price writes, "I think it is not possible for any one to conceive how bad the roads are, without seeing them. We are preserved in good health, and our minds from sinking. My mind when crossing the mountains was filled with admiration and praise in beholding the wondrous works of an Almighty hand." * * "In our preservation we have had often to exclaim, Surely these are the Lord's doings, and marvellous in our eyes. May a grateful sense thereof rest on each of our minds, to our own humiliation." "When we left *Pitt* we pursued our journey along the bank of the

Ohio, the beautiful river on the left, and on the right a mountain, with rocks overhanging our heads, awfully majestic to behold. We may say with the poet,—

> 'These are thy glorious works, Parent of good,
> Almighty! Thine this universal frame,
> Thus wondrous fair; Thyself how wondrous then;
> Unspeakable, who sitt'st above these heavens
> To us invisible, or dimly seen
> In these thy lowest works; yet these declare
> Thy goodness beyond thought, and power divine.'"

At New Garden she writes, "We attended Springfield yesterday. There is a valuable settlement of Friends here in this wilderness country, whom we feel nearly united to; and I may tell thee that I fully believe that I am in my place in coming here. Though trying to be separated from you at home, yet I feel very comfortable in being with our friends here in little cabins." At Short Creek—"I received thy first and second letters; it was a feast indeed, to get so much satisfactory information; but I have been for the most part easier about home than I could have expected, having so fully given all up to Best Protection and Direction, that I sometimes can but wonder that my mind is so relieved from anxiety about you. I am truly thankful you have been so preserved, and may we all put our trust in that preserving Arm of Power, whose care is even for the sparrow." "I have met with many choice friends and relations since I left home, to whom I feel nearly and dearly united, I trust in gospel fellowship." A P. S. to this letter reminds us of a constant habit of the writer of it which many will recollect, so that at home or abroad, no time should be lost: "If you have not sent the yarn, you need not send it till you may expect we are in Virginia, *as I do not knit fast.*" She would have had more than the sublime regret of the Emperor Titus, which has made him immortal,—"that he had lost a day." She would have regretted the loss of an hour unfilled by some useful employment.

The mails then were slow, "three weeks from Pittsburgh." Four weeks had elapsed, and no letter had reached her husband. He writes 21 of 6 mo. "My dear love: Another week has passed without hearing anything from thee, whether you have got along safely or not. I did not think I should feel so anxious about hearing; but the expectations thee gave of writing makes me feel desirous to hear from thee. I intended to think as little about thee as possible, as I was in hopes it might be a means of preserving me in patience during thy long absence, and no doubt trying journey in many respects; but I think it has been so far to the contrary that I can hardly think of anything besides. And how can it be otherwise, when thou, who hast been my companion in the nearest unity and affection for so many years, art now so far separated from me? but, being as I fully believe in the direction of Best Wisdom, I must not complain nor murmur. And I think I have resigned thee, and do still, to Divine disposal, though thou art the object of my nearest and dearest affection of all earthly enjoyments; yet I have to remember, for the trial of my faith and love, that we must part with the most near earthly tie if required; and as our blessed Lord declared, If you love anything more than me you are not worthy of me. But I have no doubt, my dear love, thou hast also thy feelings and exercises about us, and art deeply concerned for our welfare, as well as that of those thou art engaged to visit in Gospel Love. And may your labours prove beneficial to many, in strengthening the weak, in confirming the feeble-minded, and in alarming such as live too unconcernedly about that part which will endure for ever, either in happiness or in misery and woe. But if only one should be rightly awakened and warned to turn from evil ways, and thereby become converted to the truth, your labours will not be fruitless, but the blessing of Divine approbation and peace will be your crowns, if you should be again favoured to return." Further letters evince the same anxious desire to receive information from the travellers—"7 mo. 7, I have had more uneasiness and been more uncomfortable than at any time since thou left us. I have sent up to West Chester regularly *every day the stage returned*, for two weeks past;" that was twice a week; now there are three arrivals of cars and stage daily, with prospect of an increase. "My health has been improving, and I have now to work hard, which I stand better than I expected." "Our dear children are all doing well, and I am much comforted in them, as the elder ones are trying to do the best they can, and I am afraid they are almost overdoing the matter sometimes."

From Wheeling, 7 mo. 24, R. Price writes, "We have attended all the meetings of the State of Ohio, except those on the Miamies, which we have apprehended our minds released from, the state of the roads having made it impracticable to reach them." "We have taken to the wagon again, having rode on horseback through the meetings, and I have had my health much better than when at home." "After attending Plainfield monthly meeting * * we have felt our minds released from the State of Ohio." "We had meetings at the Courthouses in St. Clairsville and Wheeling." "These were indeed very weighty engagements, yet I trust they were in the ordering of Best Wisdom."

After visiting Friends at and about "Redstone," or Brownsville, the travellers again crossed the Allegheny Mountains, into Virginia. After visiting a number of meetings in this State, and holding one in the Treasury Department, Washington, and others in Maryland, they returned home. Their faithful and cheerful companion and caretaker on this journey was Samuel Schofield, of Abington, Montgomery county.

In the 4th month, 1809, Sarah Talbot and Rachel Price believed it to be their religious duty to visit Friends in Virginia, and set out on the journey accompanied by Abel Otley as their caretaker. They attended meetings through Maryland, reached Fredericksburg, Virginia,—"rode down the James river, most of the way a beautiful fertile country, which was very pleasing, after travelling through that of a contrary description;" "had a favoured meeting at Caroline;" another at Richmond, and attended the yearly meeting, and generally the meetings through Eastern Virginia, wherever they could find Friends. Their meetings in parts were "few and far between," costing great fatigue to reach them; journeys which, with bad roads and hot weather, caused "Jack" and "Hunter," favourite and well-remembered horses at home, to suffer, although friend Abel was very careful of them; with whom they say "we get along in much unity, only he is not willing to move quite as fast sometimes as we would like, but we don't fall out about it." Speaking of the horses, it may be permitted the writer, who has a grateful and lively recollection of them, to pay a tribute of respect to them and their companions then at home, and say, that they were the most faithful of servants,—doers of all work,—seldom idle, and employed alike on the farm, in the team, in social visiting, and the more serious duty of going to meeting and carrying Friends on their religious journeys; and who were never refused by their owner to a friend or relative, though the plough was left thereby to stand in the furrow.

To proceed on the journey, one result of the bad roads was that "the wagon overset, down a hill, in a steep place, but through Divine mercy (the narrator says), we were preserved from receiving much hurt; I believe a grateful sense of which covered each of our minds." "Crossing the middle and north branches of the Shenandoah—then through a fertile country inhabited mostly by Germans, with the Blue Ridge on the right hand full in view, the river winding along its side, on the left the view of the north mountain from a distance, over a considerable valley of limestone land, the road being in many places paved by nature with limestone rocks, often on edge, added to the variety of the scene, but not much to the ease of the traveller."

The religious travail and exercise on this journey were both hard and consolatory. At some places their meetings were attended by many besides Friends, "some of them perhaps from curiosity to hear women preach, who sat still, were attentive and serious, and it may be said Truth reigned over all." Meetings were also held for the blacks, "wherein Best Help was mercifully found to be near, I believe to the comforting of many of that afflicted people." "I think I never have been more feelingly sensible of being in my right place, and that I am about my Heavenly Father's business, which makes hard things easier, and sweetens the bitter cups we have to drink; but if any good be done, let it be ascribed to the Great Author of all good, and nothing to the creature, lest by self becoming exalted, I be in danger, while calling to others, of becoming a castaway myself." "The meetings for discipline were favoured seasons, there being great openness to receive counsel, the sincere-hearted were encouraged, the weak strengthened, the disobedient and forgetful warned, and the dear youth invited to forsake the vanities and delusive pleasures of this fading world, and to close in with the gracious offers of Divine love, which were mercifully extended to them. I hope some of them yielded to its holy influence so far as to form resolutions to take up their cross and follow the dear Master in the way of self-denial. Oh, may it not pass off as the morning dew!" Certain meetings of Friends "painfully exercising my mind, I was almost ready to sink under discouragement. The fathers and mothers in too many instances being too much buried in the earth, and many of the young people, as it were, flying in the air. Poor Virginia, what will become of thee! If it were not for the sake of a few righteous souls that are, I trust, interceding with the Father of mercies in the behalf of the people, the judgments that seem to be impending would not long be withheld. I have had such impressions as these; but oh, may the intercessions of those be availing, so that there may be a turning from darkness unto light, and from the power of Satan unto the Lord. Notwithstanding I have felt so much tried, I have also been thankful in believing that there is a remnant in almost every place that we have been in, that are sincere-hearted, endeavouring to live up to the principle which we profess. To these we have felt nearly united." At Lynchburg, "I received thy very acceptable letter, the contents of which were very satisfactory and strengthening. I never needed more help and encouragement than at that very time. Having had a prospect that it might be right to have a meeting with the Friends and friendly people of the town, and also with the black people there, the concern was weighty and exercising to our minds; and the contents of thy letter were so cordial and encouraging that it seemed indeed like bearing up of the hands that were ready to hang down under the weight of the exercise. Thus are the rightly yoked made a helpmeet to each other, even when far separated. The meeting for Friends was, I trust, a memorable time to many. I may say without boasting, I have never been more sensible of Divine strength being afforded,—mercifully afforded,—than in these two meetings." * * "The other meeting was large; many of the gayer class of the town's folks came in, which increased the exercise, but I believe truth was in dominion. May a grateful sense thereof be remembered to my own humiliation; ascribing all unto

Him that is mindful of his little ones, who are trusting in Him."

"I can't tell thee yet how it may be about Fairfax. I have not seen a great way before me, nor often looked much back; it requiring enough of attention to distinguish the right stepping stones to tread on in the immediate path of duty, which is the most material. I wish to go there without any formed impressions; and if we feel easy without visiting the families, it will be a release, but hope to be resigned."

The following is an extract from the letter of her husband referred to: "Thy letter was very acceptable, although it had been long written; as I am always pleased to hear from one, when absent, I so dearly love, and for whose safe getting along and welfare I feel very solicitous; and it is truly comfortable to learn you have been so far cared for and supported; and though trying baptising seasons are often your portion, the Divine arm has been underneath, and I trust will continue to preserve to the end of your journey. It is pleasing to contemplate that your faces are now turned homewards, and that the time is not very distant when we may be favoured to meet again; but hope to be preserved in patience and resignation until you can have discharged the burden that has been laid on you, so as to return with the full reward of peace, and can look back with a comfortable assurance that you have not omitted doing what was pointed out in the clear openings of duty. Notwithstanding I often feel my mind low and under much depression, I still feel strengthened to bear thy absence, beyond what I had any idea I could before thou left me, which I consider as a peculiar favour, for which I cannot be too thankful; and I much desire the dispensations I have had to pass through for many months past, may in the end work for my good, and better establishment on the everlasting rock which can never be removed; and I hope I am striving to bear with resignation and patience what further trials may be yet further allotted to prove me."

From New Market, Md., 7 mo. 26, R. Price writes, "With satisfaction I can now inform thee that we have entirely left Virginia, having got through what we had in prospect there; visited all the families of Fairfax, attended the monthly meeting there, at South Fork, Goose Creek, all to good satisfaction, though often under discouragements, feeling an entire necessity of a full reliance on that Arm of Power that is alone able to help, and without whom we can do nothing to advance the great cause of Truth and righteousness." 8 mo. 4th—"Came home, found my dear husband and family all well. With heart filled with love and gratitude to the Father and Fountain of all our mercies, in that He has been pleased to afford me a portion of that peace of mind, which the world cannot give nor take away, and is beyond the conception of the worldly wise in a state of unregeneration."

The following letter, during this absence, was written by Rachel Price, to one of her sons:

"Winchester, Va., 7 mo. 5, 1809.

"DEAR SON,—I received thy very acceptable letter at Lynchburg. It afforded me much satisfaction to find thou art willing to continue in the path of self-denial, taking up thy cross to the vain customs and fashions of the world in that place of temptations and trial (Philadelphia). Oh, may thou be favoured to stand firm now in early life, despising the shame,—having an eye to the good Pattern of plainness and self-denial, remembering for thy encouragement that he has testified, that they that acknowledge Him before men, He will also acknowledge before His Father and the Holy Angels; and mayst thou also awfully remember that He has also declared that they that deny Him before men, them He will also deny before His Father and the Holy Angels. I have often felt very anxious on thy account since I left home, seeing the very great deviations in many places of the children of well concerned Friends, from plainness and simplicity, and even good moral rectitude; but, notwithstanding this is the case with too many, yet there are some precious young people in this land of oppression, which afford a comfortable prospect of a succession in some places. And I may tell thee, for thy encouragement, that I fully believe that those that are standing firm to this profession, keeping to the principles which we profess, are much better respected by the people of the world, than those that are baulking the testimony, by giving way in dress and address; and am sure that by keeping to the principle is the alone way to obtain peace of mind here, and furnishes the only well-grounded hope of peace when time shall be no more. I am pleased to find thou art satisfied with thy place and business,—hope thou endeavours to improve in every sense of the word, so as to be capable of doing well for thyself. In endeared affection,

Thy mother,

RACHEL PRICE."

This letter is given as an instance of the anxious care extended to all the children, all of whom conformed not only in religious profession, but in respect to dress and address, except in the latter particulars the three who adopted learned professions. The term *shame* it is believed was used in reference to the feeling experienced by those who wish not to be singular and unfashionable in fashionable company. It cannot be doubted that those only can be respected by any class who act faithfully up to their own convictions of duty, whether it be in dress, address, or the more important matter of Christian faith and practice. In the advanced progress of Christianity its profession has ceased to be cause of shame or reproach, but rather the absence of a Christian faith and practice, and the caution often is, with those who are true to an honest integrity, not to profess faster than the conviction is sincerely felt; thus avoiding all just imputation of hypocrisy or of lightly handling sacred things.

The severest of trials to young Friends, when entering upon life, often is, to observe the simplicity of manners, dress, and address, of their religious Society; and the conclusion is erroneously formed that its requirings in these respects are inconsistent with a genteel training and a polished behaviour. It is true that the use of unmeaning compliments and fashionable manners would be irreconcileable with the views of Friends; but in respect to all that really constitutes the character of a true gentleman or lady, the training and principles of the Society should furnish the truest elements, in the benevolent impulses of the heart and the inculcated duty of doing unto others as we would have others do unto us, which will unquestionably imbue the feelings with a sincere kindness, and the desire to receive and return a frank courtesy and respect. Having this spring to their conduct in social intercourse, the Society of Friends has always exhibited to the world bright examples of men and women, of pure morals, polished manners, and cultivated intellects, who would have felt at home and ranked high in the most cultivated and intelligent society in any age or country of the world, provided only it should be truthful, unpretending, and virtuous. Such in England were

Penington, Ellwood, Penn, Barclay, Fothergill, Collinson, Tooke, Allen, Gurney, and Fry; and in America, Logan, Pemberton, Emlen, Savery, Dillwyn, Waln, Griffitts, Cox, Stabler, Whitall, Cope, and Parrish. The law of Christian benevolence and love should, and ever will, induce gentle, kind, and courteous manners, and all beyond is idle ceremony and useless vanity. In short, goodness and intelligence will ever lead all the true graces in their train.

In 1810, Rachel Price visited generally the meetings of the Western Quarter; and in 1812, those of Abington Quarter; with good satisfaction. In 1813, Philip Price went in company with Jesse Kersey to the Ohio Yearly Meeting, being the first held there. It was a horseback journey, and meetings were appointed by the way. The Yearly Meeting commenced with apprehensions that there would be "a want of qualified, discerning Friends, to conduct the business of so important an assembly as a yearly meeting." These apprehensions were not realized. "The meeting closed on 6th-day," writes P. Price, "and I may sum up the whole by saying it was a very satisfactory meeting. Jesse Kersey was much favoured. Indeed I never have known him more conspicuously so, or appear more in his place than in being here at this time."

Those who heard Jesse Kersey at this period of his life, will never forget the power of his eloquence. In the deliberative assemblies of the Society he would carefully observe and sympathize with the exercise of the body, and then state the views that had opened upon his own mind, with a clearness of demonstration and impressive influence that seldom, if ever, failed to guide and make the sense of the meeting conclusively apparent and satisfactory. In the meetings for worship he would commence his subject by a text or proposition, calmly and deliberately consider it, reason upon it, and support it by scriptural citation and example, and proceed by a clear, logical deduction and cogent argument; discourse of the precious gift of God to the souls of men; of that faith which is the evidence of things not seen, the substance of things hoped for; that faith which proceeds from a living principle, the light and life of the spirit, and manifests itself in corresponding works; and as himself and hearers became more deeply interested, and the sensibilities were awakened, the examples of the devoted servants of the Most High, in past ages, and of His precious visitations to all people, in all times, for their guidance and preservation, were dwelt upon, in persuasive and touching appeals to the feelings, and in tones pathetic and impressive. It was truly "the feast of reason and the flow of soul," in the highest sense, awakening to a recognition of our obligations of worship and obedience to a beneficent and merciful Creator, and of love to Him and love to our fellow-creatures. Then followed the deeply impressive silence,—eloquently impressive to an audience in tears,—owning the overshadowing spirit of the Head of the living Church of God; to be, after a precious season of fraternal love and prayerful feeling, broken by audible prayer in the same persuasive voice, of humble thankfulness and praise to the condescending Father of Mercies, for his gracious visitation to the hearts of His people; to be followed by another solemn pause and felt quietude, before the separation of the assembly. It has been acknowledged by competent judges, that within, or without, the Society of Friends, in England or America, no more gifted and impressive powers of sacred eloquence have been heard than those that proceeded from the lips of Jesse Kersey; yet his advantages of literary education had been very limited and his employment humble. But as was the plastic clay under his moulding touch, so was he himself beneath the forming hand of Infinite Goodness and Mercy.

Thus far had I written, with the design to

"No farther seek his merits to disclose,
Or draw his frailties from their dread abode,
(There they alike in trembling hope repose),
The bosom of his Father and his God."

But his own narrative has since been published, and in the sincerity of the deeply contrite and repentant heart, has disclosed the "horror of the great darkness" that fell upon him, in the use of stimulants, induced by pernicious medical treatment. In the depth of mortification and humiliation he was brought to the confession that—"among all the remedies for distress, there is none more dreadful than that of intemperance!" As an awful warning and beacon to others, this most signal downfall of the bright, the gifted, and eloquent servant of God, is probably little less useful, than if his course through life had continued in its meridian splendour, unobscured by clouds and darkness. But he again found Friends to sympathize and aid him in the effort to recover from the fearful infirmity; and the life and services of his latter years, if without their earlier strength and brightness, shed a mild and benignant light, as he sank to his final rest. It is a beautiful and instructive trait of character, that though undergoing the severest of trials, and deepest of humiliations, he indulged not in a spirit of resentment, but allowed his sufferings to be the chastening means of self-reproof and reformation. He passed into the decline of life without the persecution, but in the repentant disposition, that made the example of James Naylor, after his sad delusion and inhuman persecution, so pathetically touching. "I cannot (says Kersey) look back to the period when my standing was called in question, without feeling the most poignant remorse, that I should have been in any degree the cause of reproach to the ever blessed principle of Truth, of which I have made profession." But he turned to the great Source of true consolation to all who repent, "having witnessed that his

God was indeed a God of mercy and long-suffering kindness."

It is from the depths of extremest suffering, that often the soul is brought, through chastisement, to its most perfect state of purification and forgiveness. Of this experience, the dying declarations of James Naylor, are among the most touching and instructive to all, and beautifully illustrative of the true spirit of Quakerism and of Christianity. "There is a spirit which I feel, that delights to do no evil, nor to revenge any wrong; but delights to endure all things, in hope to enjoy its own in the end. Its hope is to outlive all wrath and contention, and to weary out all exaltation and cruelty, or whatever is of a nature contrary to itself. It sees to the end of all temptations; as it bears no evil in itself, so it conceives none in thought to any other. If it be betrayed, it bears it; for its ground and spring is the mercy and forgiveness of God. Its crown is meekness; its life is everlasting love unfeigned. It takes its kingdom with entreaty, and not with contention, and keeps it by lowliness of mind. In God alone it can rejoice, though none else regard it, or can own its life. It is conceived in sorrow, and brought forth without any to pity it; nor doth it murmur at grief and oppression. It never rejoiceth, but through sufferings; for with the world's joy it is murdered. I found it alone; being forsaken. I have fellowship therein with those who lived in dens and desolate places in the earth; who through death obtained this resurrection, and eternal, holy life."

This is that spirit that Friends so well understand, but which the world is so much at a loss to comprehend. This is that love and Gospel fellowship that drew them together and so richly compensates, even in prisons and solitary places, for all sacrifices, sufferings, and privations. It was "unto the Jews a stumbling-block, and to the Greeks foolishness,"—and even the Christian world yet but imperfectly comprehends it. The world casts its reproach because a spiritual profession, that is unfettered by the letter, may run into an extreme of license, unjustly refusing to judge by the test of the fruits, as Divinely enjoined; and it brings into question the good citizenship of a people who will not fight to sustain the laws, for their firesides, their country, and their religion. The answer would be enough for them to say, we obey God rather than man. But is it not also a just and sufficient answer for them to give, If all men lived justly and as we in peace and amity with all the world, there never would be a call to fight for law, firesides, country, or religion? Living in the example of Christ, their testimony is to be borne to all the world, and in manner irritant to none, and can only be consistently borne by a perfect abstinence from all contention and strife; and though it might be that upon occasions they should fall defenceless victims to the wicked and violent, it is but in accordance with the great example of their Spiritual Leader, in his arrest, suffering, and sublimest act of forgiveness on the cross, who forbade his servants to fight, and prayed for his enemies, "Father forgive them, for they know not what they do." No two nations, both just and wise, ever went to war. Friends' example and warning are to both and to all, and the force of that example and warning would be lost if they mingled at all in the fierceness of strife and bloodshed. Unresistant by force, they suffered torture, imprisonment, and death, by thousands, in Old England, and were whipped and hung in New England. By their patient, firm, and resolute heroism, what did they not accomplish, not for themselves only, but for all others? Inhumanity and cruelty at length relented, wearied of their persecutions, and human rights, by the fidelity and sufferings of Friends, became secured by better laws. When vested with political power in a new commonwealth, they acted not on that too common principle of our nature, that makes the slave put in power the severest taskmaster, or the persecuted in his turn the severest persecutor, as if by infliction on others to compensate for former sufferings endured. Friends in Pennsylvania were, by their toleration and justice, the admiration of the wise and good of all the world; and their pacific principle and practice, even as a worldly policy, put to shame the wisdom of the other earlier settlers on this continent. Without arms they landed among and exposed themselves to the tender mercies of those called savages. They formed a treaty of peace with them, the only one it is said ever formed without an oath, and the only one never broken; and if violated ever in spirit, it was not by the Indians so much as by those descendants and agents of the family of William Penn, who, in departing from his strict sense of justice, as they did also from his religious profession, overreached the Indians by *"long walks,"* accelerated to *running*, to encompass undue quantities of land, and hence bred a discontent and insecurity of far greater loss and disadvantage than the price that would have been cheerfully taken for the lands thus unjustly gained. And when war came by the acts of others, Friends in its midst enjoyed the highest security. It is a needless task to destroy those who will not fight—those who will not be enemies; and it is unnatural to injure those whose avocation it is to go about doing good. Few, indeed, are so wantonly cruel, certainly not the *Savages*, as to destroy known benefactors; those engaged in works of love and charity; in helping the helpless, relieving the destitute, healing the wounded, curing the sick, visiting the imprisoned; such as the Howards, the Frys, the Dixes, or those most devoted of women, the "Sisters of Charity," who frequent the wards of pestilence and death, to minister to the sick and dying. Prejudice, passion, and wickedness, may be inflamed and for a time triumph, and inflict penalties and punishment upon the disinterested benefactors of the helpless victims of oppression, or of the insane inmates of their asylums, and burn the convents of harmless women who have devoted their lives to religion; but the reacting sentiment of humanity and justice will soon again restore the unjustly injured to their true position of respect, favour, and gratitude.

But if the peace principle held by Friends, be impracticable as a worldly policy, it is only so because of the injustice and wickedness of the world. And is that a sufficient motive for them to abandon their heavenly descended principle, and to succumb to and participate in that injustice and wickedness? Is it not rather their duty ever and unflinchingly to maintain their sacred testimony against evils of man's self-infliction so cruel, brutal, and devastating, as those of war? Let them not be discouraged; the world has advanced, and been advanced by them, in toleration, justice, mercy, and forgiveness. The axe, the halter, and the sword, are of less frequent application; and peace, security, and happiness, are progressive on the earth.

Be it that Friends must endure the charge of transcendentalism; it is but an assertion that their standard is excellent above that which unregenerate men have yet attained. It is but a confession that these have found Christianity impracticable to themselves. Is then the exalted standard of Christianity to be reduced to meet man's short-comings, and conform to his imperfect standard? Rather let men look upward to the standard of highest perfection, and in aiming to reach it, attain a higher excellence. Striking is the contrast between the Christian standard-bearer and his accusers. These reproach him for striving for an exalted purity, and becoming, perhaps, a martyr to principle; but he regards them with kindness, pity, charity, and forgiveness; because they know not what is their loss. They would drag him down to their worldly condition and spirit of contention; he, in abounding love and sympathy, would raise them to the enjoyment of his own pure and exalted serenity, love, and happiness, and prays that they may be forgiven, "for they know not what they do."

Yet there exists a soldiery, and it may be a patriotic soldiery, and as the world now is, the necessary protectors of order and security, but they are a necessity arising only from the wickedness or folly of mankind, and to be used, in worldly policy, in the smallest practicable quantity, as themselves dangerous to security and liberty. But looking to the ultimate good, and to the influence of the advocates of peace on that public opinion that determines the momentous question of peace or war, these are to be cherished as affording that example, and the maintainers of that principle, which alone can mirror and establish the future pervading happiness of the world, that is the hope of all good men. Thus, if in the minority, they accomplish a great good; and could they obtain a unanimity of sentiment and practice, then would the world witness an unprecedented peace and prosperity,—even the bliss fabled by poets, and the happiness hoped for in the millennium. But if the ultimate perfection and happiness be unattainable, yet is every approach a gain to the world; while to those who are of the kingdom whose "servants fight not," it is a realized beatitude, except only as the good must ever sympathize with and strive for the recovery of the unregenerate and uninstructed in their own true felicity.

During the second war with England, from 1812 to 1815, when foreign supplies were cut off, our own manufacturers having a monopoly of the home market, Merino sheep came into great request, and attained highly speculative prices. Large flocks then and afterwards ranged the farms of Philip Price, and were good fertilizers of the soil. But with the influx brought by the return of peace, of foreign goods, and the impolitic abandonment by the government of an adequate protection to the capital invested in manufactories, wool and sheep found a sudden depression, and the loss on these aggravated the difficulties of the farming interests, otherwise severely suffering under the fall of prices incident to a return after the war from an inflated paper currency to a specie basis. The large flocks that whitened the hills of Chester county soon disappeared, only to reappear, many years afterwards, on the cheaper lands of the rolling surface of Washington and adjoining counties in western Pennsylvania. An incident occurred in relation to the produce of the sheep of P. Price, that afforded some amusement at the time. Until then blue had been the standing military colour, and he had his wool manufactured into gray cloth and sent to the store at West Chester, thinking it quite secure from military service; but it so happened that the first volunteer company there formed fancied that colour, called themselves the "Chester County Grays," and the writer, then a lad in the store, thought himself in good luck to sell the whole stock of Quaker cloth to the members to go to camp. The companies at Marcus Hook were not, however, called to meet the enemy, and the clothing had only served to keep the soldiers warm, a circumstance hardly to be regretted, since among them were personal friends, and an uncle of the writer, Joseph H. Brinton, who, though of great wealth, advanced age, and mild manners, believed it to be his duty to turn out as a volunteer private in the defence of his country. He was not bred a Friend, and was undoubtedly actuated by a high sense of patriotic feeling.

The Agricultural Society of Chester county was organized early in the year 1820, by the election of Philip Price, as President, Doctor William Darlington, as Vice-President, and Isaac Sharpless, as Secretary; and about fifty of its most substantial and worthy farmers were appointed on its ten committees. It was the first society in the State composed chiefly of practical farmers. The objects embraced by its standing committees, evince the intelligence and liberal scope of the minds of the members. The committees were: 1. On farm buildings, fences, and implements of husbandry; 2. On the veterinary art; 3. On natural history, particularly mineralogy and entomology; 4. Political economy; 5. Domestic animals; 6. Grasses, grains, and roots; 7. Manures; 8. Fruit and forest trees; 9. Irrigation and draining; 10. Horticulture; with specifications of the objects and purposes of each committee. An address to the citizens of the county was prepared by Nathan H. Sharpless, recommending its objects, and inviting investigation and contribution of the results of experiment and experience; which states that "it is within the memory of many of us that this county was very poor, but thanks to the worthy founders of our present farming system, our own industry and a beneficent Providence, it has arisen to a degree of prosperity and excellence seldom witnessed in so short a period of time. Most of you know how this has been accomplished. It has been effected by a judicious rotation of crops, by clover and gypsum." To encourage the diffident and unpractised with the pen, the address proceeds,—"It would not be expected that all communications, to be beneficial, should be grammatically correct, or in smoothly rounded periods;

practical observations and facts, tending in any degree to illustrate the subject, will find as ready acceptance dressed in the plainest language of simplicity, as the more polished sentences of the philosopher or scholar." A further address, from the pen of another member, William H. Dillingham, will also be found in the columns of the "Village Record," of the same year, enforcing concert of action for the common interest, the diffusion of useful intelligence, and to raise the profession of agriculture in the public estimation. Much of this address would have been forcibly pertinent in favour of the formation of a State Agricultural Society, as lately consummated, at a central point for exhibition, the receipt and diffusion of information, seeds, &c. And reference is made to another great branch of human industry to enforce the argument and afford encouragement to a like vigilance and concentration of power. "In no part of the world are the merchants without their Chamber of Commerce, and to this means, in a great measure, is to be ascribed, not only their high respectability as a body, but their great unanimity in public measures, and their weight in almost every government. The moment their interests are touched in any one point, the whole body sympathizes, and all their influence is exerted through the common organ." Chester county has now her Horticultural Hall, and though a later architectural ornament to West Chester than the Chester County Cabinet, the liberal scope of the purposes of the Agricultural Society probably suggested the formation of the Cabinet, Horticultural Society, &c. Certain, however, it is, that such naturalists as Dr. Darlington, David Townsend, Joshua Hoopes, and many others, were active in all, and by their industry and zeal, have added to the scientific character of the county, and one of them by his publications has acquired a reputation among European savans. In giving his own learning, and the remains of other naturalists — of a Baldwin, Marshall, Collinson, and Bartram—to the public, he has acted in the benevolent spirit, and not in that of those whom Buckminster reproaches as the misers of learning, who hoard for themselves alone: "That learning, whatever it may be, which lives and dies with the possessor, is more worthless than his wealth, which descends to posterity." If all capable of teaching would thus earnestly devote themselves in some way and to some extent, to instruct mankind, the progress of improvement would be vastly accelerated.

During the years of their superintendence of West-Town, and afterwards of their school at West Chester, the duties there devolved upon them, relieved Philip and Rachel Price from the service of distant travel. Their sphere of influence was, however, hardly more circumscribed. Children came to them from far and near, to experience from them the care and concern of earthly parents, and to sit under the teaching of a spiritual mother. The communion of feeling was promotive of the mutual happiness; for they loved the innocence and purity of youth, untainted by a knowledge of the evils of the world, and drew them unto them in the spirit of the Holy one, who said "suffer little children to come unto me, and forbid them not, for of such is the kingdom of Heaven." Meetings of worship were regularly held in the house at West-Town; and besides an attendance at the places of worship, frequent family sittings, and readings of the Scriptures of Truth, took place in the school, at West Chester. On such occasions, and to her latest age of over eighty years, Rachel Price spoke under emotions of deep humility and exercise of religious feeling, as in the discharge of a duty she could not disobey and obtain the peace of mind her soul coveted. Her power of voice was not great, but gentle and pathetic in its tones, and sweetly in unison with the affectionate appeals made to her hearers. She ever dwelt upon the Divine precepts of our Saviour,—His love, His sufferings, and sacrifice, with an intense sympathy and love, inducing a like feeling of love and appreciation of His merits in others. She ever held in view His promise to return as the Comforter and spiritual visiter to the souls of men; admonishing the young to heed His gentle knockings at the door of the heart, and the whisperings of the still small voice of love, offering its divine counsels for safe guidance through a world beset with temptations. Though it should demand continual watchfulness, and the road be straight and narrow, yet it was with the promise that all His ways were ways of peace, and all His paths paths of pleasantness. With more than the yearning of a mother's affection, she would gather them beneath the enfolding wings of Gospel love. It is believed that she was seldom visited with the sorrowful regret of Him who wept over the people of Jerusalem, whom He would thus have gathered, "but they would not;" but it is remembered with contrition by one of her sons, who had absented himself from her on an occasion of religious worship, that the solemn language came sorrowfully to her mind in reference to him,—"Couldst not thou watch one hour" with me? The keenest of reproaches, communicated in love, was followed, as in the Divine example, by a benign forgiveness. With the stricken and disconsolate she was deeply sympathetic, and most affectionate in her appeals that they should turn to the true and everlasting source of comfort; and often did she repeat to such the invitation of the Divine Master, with the sanction of her own heartfelt experience,—"Come unto me, all ye that labour and are heavy laden, and I will give you rest. Take my yoke upon you, and learn of me; for I am meek and lowly in heart; and ye shall find rest unto your souls; for my yoke is easy, and my burden is light."

At no period of life, and under no circumstances, did

the children of these affectionate parents cease to be the objects of their Christian care and deep parental solicitude. Those who adopted professions, did so not under a prohibition, yet without their "cordial approbation." In the legal profession, it was apprehended, there could be little quiet peace of mind to be enjoyed, in the midst of strife and contention; that temptation would arise to make causes appear difficult to enhance the fees; and that while "sensible there is no profession by which a man may raise himself in the public estimation more conspicuously, it might lead away from that true Christian dignity which is so much superior to all this world can confer. Though the happiness and comfort of my beloved children has always been an object of my most ardent desire, and I have endeavoured to promote it as far as was in my power, and have wished to leave them very much to choose for themselves such occupations as would accord with their own views, yet I have always desired they might be content with the humble walks of life, in which there is much less temptation to depart from those principles which we must practise, if ever we expect to secure that peace and felicity which can only be attained thereby." * * "Notwithstanding we have been much comforted in a belief that thou hast intended to regulate thy conduct by the strictest integrity and morality, fears will be excited from thy continual exposure" to adverse influences. This is an instance of repeated expressions of parental regard and wisdom of one of the best of fathers, pointing to the true sources of human happiness and dignity. One rule given by him at the outset of professional practice, cannot be too often inculcated on young beginners,—"always to have the client's money ready when he calls."

While the subjects of this memoir were always friendly to the cause of education, and devoted much of their lives to its promotion, it was in regard to the education of the heart that they were ever most solicitous. They well understood the risk there constantly is that the learning of the head may be at the expense of that teaching of the heart which it was the great and unceasing purpose of their lives to foster. In regard to those sons who had chosen the learned professions, their anxiety in this respect was intense, and their warnings frequent and solemn. They perceived the danger incurred of a yielding to the suggestions of an absorbing ambition, and that even the laudable desire of being sufficiently learned to be skilful and reliable, might exact so much time and so fully occupy the mind, as to become too exclusive an engagement, and leave the more precious seed and germs of the heart to wither, exhausted of their needful support. Ambition they knew to be a barren soil for the growth of the gentle affections, and the reasoning faculty they believed often to be impoverishing to the growth of religious life. Besides the exacting demands of professional learning and business, the scholar who too exclusively cultivates and relies upon the deductions of his understanding is ever in peril of placing an undue dependence upon his own intellectual strength and moral fortitude. The observation of physical facts and close logical deductions become engagements too exclusive to permit a corresponding culture of the moral and religious susceptibilities with which we are wonderfully endowed. The self-confident philosopher assumes the problem of life to be, and he the wisest man, who can derive the greatest amount of pleasurable sensations with the fewest of pain: the laws of health are to be observed to avert pain and suffering; but consistently therewith pleasure may be tasted to the measure of the human capacity for enjoyment. This theory, adopted in the ardour and confidence of youth in its practical carrying out, is commonly found to be depreciative of worth and character; indulgence begets increase of appetite; the Stoic gives way to the Epicurean philosophy; and the pride of intellectual strength must succumb in sympathetic decay with the undermined physical powers. The sentinel Reason, in dalliance with pleasure, is betrayed and lost to the enemy, and is powerless to retrieve the fatal error, or reascend the way so easy of declension.

Against the ever operative seductions of the sensual appetites, producing a moral paralysis and spiritual inanity, as well as destructive to health, Christianity teaches, and Friends have ever emphatically preached, a sure means of preservation and safety to every human soul. It instructs to the observance of a higher principle of action, cultivates to a higher sensibility to virtue, a quicker perception of evil, and to an appreciation of higher joys, in the presence of which degrading vices cease to tempt, and, become repulsive, now confirm virtuous resolves. Friends find in the promises of the Gospel, and in the experiences of their own spiritual travail, a quicker monitor than the process of reason; for reason short-sightedly estimates the tempting pleasure at a value that will ever bias the decision, while in the sacrifice of it the far-seeing Christian soldier finds in his triumph a more than compensating foretaste of a superior happiness. Friends have been the especial instructors in the doctrine of the inward guide and Divine light "given to every man to profit withal," and ever nigh, "even in the heart." They experimentally know that "The heart of the wise teaches his mouth and addeth learning to his lips." It is the doctrine of the Scriptures, every part of which gleams with the truth that God speaks to and operates upon the hearts of his people. It comports with His beneficence and justice towards the creatures of his own creation that He should cast a light on their path, through the perilous pilgrimage of life; and it is not for philosophy to assert that the Master of all causes cannot shape them to His ends, influence the affections, change the heart, and suggest the thoughts of men, for their individual or national guidance. The Psalmist exclaims, "Whither shall I go from Thy spirit? or whither shall I flee from Thy presence?" "I will praise Thee, for I am fearfully and wonderfully made." "How precious also are *Thy Thoughts* unto me, oh, God! How great is the sum of them! If I should count them, they are more in number than the sand: When I awake, I am still with Thee." And how emphatic and awfully impressive, and repressive of sinful indulgences, the declarations of the New Testament, "Know ye not that ye are the temple of God, and that the spirit of God dwelleth in you?" and "if any man defile the temple of God, him shall God destroy:" "The kingdom of heaven is within;" and "the fruit of the Spirit is love, joy, peace, faith."

Those who are quiescent from agitating worldly influences, desirous to be enlightened, and guided by the highest wisdom, sincerely true to their own happiness and prayerfully earnest that they might not be betrayed into temptation, cannot have failed to perceive feelings to arise and thoughts to be suggested of unwonted clearness, as obeyed to conduce to safety of conduct and solace of mind; and again in the retrospects of the future, the Divine guidance through the besetting perils of the past, but become more conspicuously apparent, in the visible shipwrecks of others, with which the shores of life are strewn. Man may do much to put himself in the position to be the recipient, but cannot of his own will command, the Divine favour : He may withdraw himself from the current of worldly cares and strifes, enter into his closet, or gather among those of whom Christ has promised to be in the midst, and patiently waiting, "in the silence of all flesh," he will find precious visitations to his soul, coming unbidden and without human effort, and often without discernible association according to any asserted law regulating the successions of human thought. Holy influences are breathed upon the soul more sweetly than the tones of music, potent to dispel its anxieties, kindling into faith, hope, and joy. Though the understanding be not able to trace the cause or comprehend the means of operation, the effect and the fact are obviously apparent. The presence of a power of spiritual discernment is felt, and its discernments are perceived with sufficient distinctness to become the practical and sure guidance of life. "The wind bloweth where it listeth, and thou hearest the sound thereof, but canst not tell whence it cometh or whither it goeth; so is every one that is born of the spirit." Judging from the beneficent effects, it is enough to believe its source is good and its end peace and happiness. This Divine influence, figuratively called "the light within," so earnestly believed and preached by ancient Friends as to become their most distinguishing characteristic, is that doctrine most prominently taught in all the Scriptures of Truth, and owning the inward and operative presence of the Spirit of God is most potent to purge of sin and give elevation and purity to the human affections. Who, dwelling in this faith, can dare to pollute the chosen temple of the Immaculate, to dim its heavenly lustre, and crucify again the Holy Spirit in this inward appearance!

This doctrine, preached and practised by all true Friends, and most consistently preached and practised through life by the subjects of this Memoir, is, however, ever accompanied by the warning that the voice that speaks within may be unheeded until it shall not speak again; that the eye may be so wilfully closed upon the light as to become sealed in blindness. This voice may speak in whispers, but in stillness is to be listened to and obeyed; and though the light appear as the earliest dawn, yet is it to be watched to its perfect day. The faith begotten is in the beginning compared to the smallest of seed, which may grow to great size; but its germ, however small, is not to be choked, nor the flower of promise crushed, or there will be no fruit. The good seed is broadly cast upon every soil, as the rain is sent alike upon the just and the unjust, that none may have excuse; but with some it falls as upon stony places, with others as among thorns, and with some as upon good ground. The duty and responsibility is with the recipient to give it nourishment and growth until it shall yield good fruit: It may be quickened by the tears of repentant sorrow, or by those that spring from the grateful heart of love and devotion, alike owning its source, the "living water springing up into everlasting life."

This growth, though "it cometh without observation," is as certain and visible in its effects upon human feelings, thought, conduct, and character, as the phenomena of physical nature, and thus carries with it the same force of demonstration. Philosophy itself enumerates "the principle of faith" and "the sense of the Deity" as inherent in the human mind;* whilst it also avers the sources of all human ideas to proceed from sensation, and the reflective operations of the mind.† But these are perceived and known only by *consciousness;* nay, it is only by consciousness that we know that we live and recognise our own identity; and it is equally by consciousness that the spiritual operations are felt and known, than which, and the religious convictions thereby sealed upon the mind, nothing can be more direct and powerful. There is no evidence of higher certainty that can reach the human understanding; all must reach the mental consciousness; it is *experience* all, perceived, felt, known experience.

With, therefore, all the certainty of demonstration that pertains to objects of physical perception, is it not rational to believe that the Creator should ever be as operative upon human feeling, thought, and conduct, as that His power should be incessantly active upon all the

* Rush on the Mind, 10. † Locke, Stewart.

inferior creation? All things proclaim their origin in a Supreme Intelligence, whose watchfulness and protection are never for a moment intermitted; and man, the highest in perfection, and of greatest permitted range and liberty of choice, most of all needs guidance and protective care, and must mainly receive and share it through the feelings and mental operations. No one will rationally say that a being so wonderfully framed and mentally endowed as man is the production of blind, physical causes,—in structure, feeling, immaterial thought and heavenly aspirations,—of causes absolute, irreversible, unvaryingly and eternally operative—without subsequent interposition to imbue a feeling or suggest a thought for mortal guidance. This would contradict the beneficence and wisdom displayed in all creation. Man's wants are infinitely diversified, and as infinite the resources must be for his well being. Is it a greater marvel to the comprehension that God should regard and protect in the enjoyment of life and happiness, the being whom he created, than that he should have especially interposed to create him? Whom he did create and does perpetuate by mysteriously preserving the equality of the sexes, and by providing the resources of food and raiment, is it extraordinary that he should mentally and spiritually guide? All things tell us that God hath done all things well, and nothing in vain. He has endowed the moral nature, and gives the spiritual discernment and impulse to prayer. Shall he then clothe the lily in its beauty, and give to all vital nature the impulse and direction appropriate to its prescribed development, and yet shall He not inspire the grateful heart in its worship and praise to Him? Yes, truly, "the preparation of the heart in man and the answer of the tongue are from the Lord." He is that "friend that sticketh closer than a brother." To whom then He bids to knock, will he not open the door? to whom to implore will He not give? Of Him that knoweth what things we have need of before we ask, shall we not "find grace to help in time of need?" It is true He must be the Judge of what we need, and we shall not receive what we unwisely ask; but asking in submission to His will, shall ever receive contentment and peace, and attain that condition wherein best we deserve and are most certain to receive suggestion and aid for our relief and well-being. Then it is we most certainly come into a conformity with the Divine will, and into the condition best to subserve human happiness. Then it is that the disturbing interests and passions become allayed, the understanding cleared, and the voice of wisdom is heard, inevitably suggestive of improvement, safety, and happiness; and then it is that assailing temptations vanish, as evil spirits into their dark abodes, the soul becomes purified, and the apprehensive anxiety ever mingling in our mysterious existence is appeased, and we come to know a reconciliation with our Heavenly

Father. Then in another and happier sense we find verified the pristine declaration of Jehovah, "My spirit shall not always strive with man;" but strive it ever assuredly will, so long as aught exists at variance with it, until there be a submission and conformity, or the lost soul becomes hardened and deaf to the voice of Divine instruction. For those who have "tasted the good word of God and of the powers of the world to come," may "fall away," not "to renew them again unto repentance."

Have the preceding views been unduly extended, or indeed wholly misplaced? They have appeared to the writer to be applicable for the correction of a too prevalent tendency of the learned mind, and to be a just acknowledgment to the wisdom of the parental solicitude, after the experience and reflection furnished by maturity of years, by one who was the object of their deep concern and anxiety. The truthful beauty and efficacy of their faith, by time and experience, have become more convincingly apparent. This corrective experience has in a degree involved the task of unlearning what had been learned, and of retracing the divergent steps to come to the more simple path from whence the departure was taken. It is a retrograde course that philosophy and learning are ever compelled to take, to test elaborate and overwrought theory by that which is unsophisticated, unbiassed, and simply truthful. When the pride of learning has overlooked and travelled beyond the simple evidences of truth within the mind, and a literal theology has darkened knowledge and disregarded the very fountain of true religious faith and experience—a recurrence to a simpler test becomes necessary; and this service the Society of Friends rendered to the world in its rise and subsequent existence. It called upon mankind to turn their minds inward to observe the manifestations of truth and wisdom, there to be perceived, felt, and understood, with the certainty of sensation, and the clearness of a self-evident proposition, showing, by a light always at hand, a way so clearly that even the simple may find and not err therein. The sincere and honest mind could never find it difficult to distinguish the presence and pervasive influence of feelings and thoughts infused in every crisis restraining from evil, from those of an opposing nature, betraying into the besetting temptation. The difficulty ever was to draw the attention of men from the attractions and disturbance of outward and worldly influences, from agitating passions and deceptive reasonings, to an observance of this simple but purest and sublimest source of teaching, which, if faithfully begun and persevered in, with a just fidelity to its manifestations, and a proper regard to their own happiness, would be found to experience a larger growth, obtain a predominance and victory over gross and earthly propensities, and productive of feelings and thoughts so elevated and enlightened as to be in themselves a source of inexpressible satisfaction, and thus minister to the soul the evidences of a Divine approval and authority.

A rigid and sceptical philosophy will call this experience but an enthusiastic feeling: it is, nevertheless, a reality, in itself happiness, instructive in the highest intelligence, and has all, and more than all, of the evidence that is the basis of philosophical demonstration. It is evidenced by consciousness, by the deductions of the rational power of the understanding, by its good fruits, and more than earthly felicity. Those who have this happy experience "have tasted of the heavenly gift," and learned that of a certainty "the true worshippers shall worship the Father in spirit and in truth." This heavenly teaching and spiritual worship is a source of instruction alike open to the illiterate and the learned; for to all, in the infinite beneficence of the Almighty Father, a portion of His blessed spirit is imparted, in measure sufficient, if obeyed, to lead into righteousness, to interpret the Holy Scriptures, lend to their perusal a holy joy, and unerringly guide into His everlasting rest. This belief, and this alone, can keep the mind directed heavenward, and its rejection, to set it towards a material philosophy, that is "of the earth, earthy," that must bring it to a spiritual death, and the sacrifice of the most exalted affections and aspirations of the human soul. All that there is of pleasure in appetites and propensities repressed and supplanted by this Heavenly influence, is more than compensated here on earth by the pure and holy joy it dispenses at all times and in all places, whether in the busy throngs of the world's progressions, or in the silence of solitude and night, whilst the blessed promises for the future life are illimitably consoling and beatific. The innocent and the good alone are happy, but most truly so when man fully enjoys his pre-eminent privilege to love and adore his Creator. This most exalted service of the human mind, neither rejects nor disparages any intellectual faculty, but, in deep humility, every holy feeling and every power of the understanding is submissively engaged in the adoration of the Infinite in power and wisdom.

That the vicious should disbelieve in the intercession of the spirit of God, and in His divine inspiration, is natural, for they will stifle that which whets the conscience to turn its sharpened edge upon all their iniquity. That philosophers should doubt, proceeds from another and too exclusive occupation and reliance of the mind, withdrawing its attention from a watchful perception of and submission to God's best gift to man, in its cherished growth constituting man's highest excellence and perfection of character. But that professing Christians and Christian teachers should call in question this great saving Truth, without which all religion loses its vitality, is matter of marvel, and only to be comprehended in the admission of the fact that such outward and literal views are taken by them as to turn the perception and intellect from the true source of Divine enlightenment and religious conviction. The Scriptures assure us of the visitations of the spirit of the Almighty to the souls of men in ancient days; that it strove with man; that "in the beginning was the Word—and the Word was God:" He raised up prophets in all ages, and they addressed themselves to that which was spiritual in man. He declared to Israel, "I will pour my spirit on thy seed." Has the human race, then, become less the object of Divine regard? Did Christianity introduce a less spiritual dispensation? or did it more especially and emphatically call man to a recognition of the spiritual coming of Christ again? It declares, "A man can receive nothing unless it be given him of Heaven." "Unto every one of us is given grace, according to the measure of the gift of Christ." And Jesus said, "I will pray the Father, and he shall give you another comforter, that he may abide with you for ever;" "the spirit of Truth will guide you into all Truth;" and thus the New Testament abounds in blessed promises. The kingdom of God is declared to be within; and that without a new birth, man cannot see the kingdom of God. He must be born of the spirit, "and that which is born of the spirit is spirit." This regeneration then comes of God, and is the manifestation of His Holy spirit upon the soul of man. But wherefore, unless He can change the disposition of the heart, inspire holier feelings and infuse better thoughts, and thus speak to and inspire man's highest intelligence and guide his course on earth? If there be a spark of religion in the human breast, it is there Divinely lighted, and for a holy purpose. It must enlighten and direct. It must do so as needed; and will, as the star of night, guide the voyager in life in the hour of trouble, darkness, and peril, if he will but turn to it with faith and hope. "This God is our God, for ever and ever; he will be our guide even unto death."

This subject has not been dwelt upon without ample knowledge of the occasion for it. It was the deep concern of devoted parents, and it is fitting that it should be transmitted, as perhaps the most valuable legacy of the writer to his own children. The world has recently been shocked by the annunciation that even cultivated woman, forgetful of what seems almost the instincts of her better nature, disclaims that Gospel that alone has given her station and elevation; nay, atheistically rejects a God, and resolves all nature into "a system of ever working forces, producing forms, uniform in certain lines and largely various in the whole, and all under the operation of *immutable law.*" In her philosophy, all revelation—all spiritual influence, is a delusion; all prayer is powerless, weakness, and folly. But who established this immutable law, and empowered it to fashion all things in admirable beauty of design and perfection, is not explained. Did an immutable law produce those "forms," and breathe into them life? Did inert matter, by a spontaneous working force, take upon itself motion, and life, and thought? or did one living species produce another? All observation has shown that one species cannot generate another, and that each, in infinite number, was the object of the special interpositions of the Creative Power. Indeed, all life, in all its processes, can only be referred to the continuing action of creative power—no philosophy sounds its mysterious depth. That Book of the Almighty, to whose printed pages, at least, this unsexed philosopher will give her credence—the long-treasured archives of geology—would appear to show many successive interpositions to place differing species of animals on earth.

But such a philosophy finds its condemnation in the inherent repulsion of the human mind itself. The mind is formed to infer and believe that all things made in transcendent beauty and perfection, have had a beneficent and intelligent Author; and those who falter in this belief, are illogical exceptions to the Divine purpose. It is formed to admire the manifestations of the Divine wisdom and power, and to love, worship, and adore a Supreme Intelligence; and when it fails in this, its error is demonstrated in a failure to attain its own highest excellence and truest happiness. Thus the test of experience falsifies the philosophy. If, indeed, all results proceed from material causes, under self-existent laws of uniform operation, then must we but worship matter, and yet blindly bow down in heathen idolatry. Then must there be no spiritual future, no continuous identity of being, no righteousness nor sin, no virtue nor crime. Then is man's freedom coercion, his choice a necessity; and all matter, all life, all mind, have been predestined by laws of blind physical compulsion. This necessary reduction flagrantly exposes the falsity of the premises. It is the extreme of incongruity to assume that mind can originate from matter. Intelligence alone can produce intelligence; and the human soul ever owns the divinity of its source in its lofty desires and devotional aspirations.

The error of such a theory is, however, the less dangerous, since the mind by an instinctive dread shrinks from its adoption. But there is a more insidious danger that has always produced a watchful distrust in Friends. It is the philosophy of the schools as taught from standard works of approved character; and a system of instruction that developes the intellect more than it cultivates the affections of the heart. Turn, for instance, to the work of Locke on the Understanding, ascribing all ideas to the sources of sensation and reflection, with so rigid a severity, as to leave but the conclusion that the spirit of piety and a divine inspiration into the minds of men is but a delusive enthusiasm or hallucination of the enkindled imagination. Though himself a Christian professor, and making no ostensible attack upon religion, the tendency of his principal work is to encourage the philosophy of materialism, and is accordingly so cited and relied upon. To look to its practical effects, no one can doubt that, if fully adopted, it must quench those feelings and chill that fervour from which great actions and exalted character usually spring. If George Fox could in his youth have read the then unwritten work of his great contemporary, when first visited by those strong impressions—"that day-spring from on high"—that decided the course and character of his momentous life, and had adopted its conclusions, his religious ardour and indomitable resolution would have been for ever repressed, and his glorious mission been lost to mankind. The characters of these two great men cannot be compared by the strong contrasts of the lights and shades that discriminate the good and the bad; but by their appreciation of the enjoyment and value of life as tested by the final and truthful testimony that ends all experience, let us judge which of two good men had the truest view of the purpose and destiny of God's crowning work of creation. The philosopher, when he last received the sacrament "with fervour and piety," declared it as his final testimony, "That life appeared to him mere vanity." The preacher and reformer, when in the portal of death, opening to the vista of heavenly light and glory, whispered to surrounding friends his still progressive and triumphing experience—"All is well: the seed of God reigns over all, and over death itself. The power of God is over all, and the seed reigns over all disorderly spirits." "He died," says Penn, an attendant witness, "rejoicing in the hope of the Gospel," and must have felt that life to him had been full of deepest import, and himself the gifted instrument of inappreciable service to mankind. He must have felt, as he had ever most earnestly preached, that the lives of all are of momentous significance, as their tenor might influence human welfare on earth, or determine their future happiness or wo. If, indeed, the end of this life ended all things to individual consciousness, then, truly, life would "appear to be mere vanity;" its mingled draughts of joys and sorrows not worth the tasting; its scope and end without ennobling purpose or adequate design. But, regarded in reference to its immortal destiny, and its sojourn here as a stage of probationary trial, every emotion and experience of life but manifests creative wisdom; happiness and joy are the gifts of His beneficent bounty; pain and sorrow the vindications of His violated laws, or the purifying preparations for the felicity of heaven.

The briefest summary of the philosophy of Locke, is, that there are no innate ideas; that all ideas are derived by sensation, through the external senses, and by reflection, or the mind's own elaborations of the previously perceived sensations. The materialists thence infer that as sensation is owing to organized life, and the ideas that constitute thought and mind are thence derived; so these depend upon the material organization, and must cease with its dissolution. But their fallacy is in overlooking the fact that it is something else than the material senses that receives and acts upon the perceived sensation; that without the percipient mind had been first placed in the organized body, no sensation could be conducted to it; that its presence must precede the first and faintest perception of even fœtal infancy. *That* capacity must be innate, and, with the gift of life, come from the Creator. Then, again, the power of the percipient mind to act upon the perceived sensations, to compare, combine, analyze, infer, reason, and reflect, whence comes it? Certainly not from the external sensations; these are but channels of information to the pre-existent mental capacity, but not themselves creative of that capacity; they may enrich its resources, but are not itself. The image of external objects pictured on the retina of the eye, the sounds that vibrate on the tympanum of the ear, nor yet the impressions made upon the sense of smell, the taste, or touch, reach the mind in material essence; neither can the mental perception or thoughts evolved be material products. The nerves that serve the senses, and again obey the will, transmit no material thing to be perceived or constitute thought. And again, there are feelings, affections, hopes, fears, passions, and emotions, inherent in the human constitution, perceived of the mind, productive of thought, determinative of conduct and character. These, as well as the intellect, give to man his elevation above all the rest of animated nature. His religious susceptibility—his spiritual perception—it is that make him sensitive to the breathings of Divine Love, and bring him into the presence and under the operative teachings of the Spirit of God. These precious visitations of grace to the soul are as gratefully felt and certainly heard, as by the outward sensation the breeze that stirs the leafy grove, or wakes the Æolian chord to music; but, it may also be, to the guilty conscience, that His voice shall be heard as in the storm and in the thunder of His lightnings. Yet is it the voice of God, whether heard in vindicatory punishment, or in whisperings of peace and comfort to the contrite and repentant, or when prompting to missions of blessed charities and Gospel love. All that is good must come from the Source of all goodness, whether in disciplinary correction or in the overflow of the fountain of goodness and mercy.

Let it be understood, however, that Friends do not discourage the acquisition of knowledge to any extent that the human capacity can truthfully develope it. It is only when the incessant occupation, or the sceptical spirit in which it may be pursued, tends to obstruct the growth of the precious seed of religious faith and feeling in the heart, that the pursuit is discountenanced. They fear not but that every truthful disclosure of the operations of nature will reveal the wisdom and goodness of the Creator, and, rightly understood, will prompt the tribute of praise and adoration to Him. Philosophy then becomes the handmaid of religion, and ministers to a more exalted demonstration; expels from an impure and unintelligent faith its superstitions and weakness, and permits the unclouded understanding to perceive the power and majesty of the Creator, and the heart of devotion to worship in the confiding faith of the goodness and mercy of God. But philosophy, without religion, is to the moral and religious susceptibilities, what the arctic snows are to the world, the blighting cause of a perpetual sterility; but with religion's warmth and genial feelings as the temperate zones, equally distant from the icy coldness of unbelief and the scorching heats of fanatic zeal and persecution, clothing life and character with consistency and beauty, and productive of blessed fruits. Light and knowledge, as means intrusted, will enhance the responsibility of a faithful stewardship, but without vital warmth and earnest purpose, in religious faith and Christian charities, cannot save. The faithless to these high gifts bury even the ten talents intrusted for improvement and increase, and from such even that he hath shall be taken away.

Men of the highest range of thought and success in philosophical attainment, have pursued their studies under the influence of a devout and prayerful spirit.

When the great task of forming the constitution of the United States hung in suspense from the prevalence of discordant views, the venerable Franklin moved that the favour of Heaven should be invoked, and the differences were composed. Sir Humphry Davy, in describing the qualifications of one so materially engaged as the chemical philosopher, says—"his mind should always be awake to devotional feeling; and in contemplating the variety and beauty of the external world, and developing its scientific wonders, he will always refer to that Infinite Wisdom, through whose beneficence he is permitted to enjoy knowledge. He will rise at once in the scale of intellectual and moral existence; his increased sagacity will be subservient to a more exalted faith, and in proportion as the veil becomes thinner through which he sees the causes of things, he will admire more and more the brightness of the Divine Light, by which they are rendered visible." Dr. Rush, in the same spirit, entered upon his Inquiry into the Diseases of the Mind—as if "about to tread on consecrated ground," and thus prayerfully begins the task, "I am aware of its difficulty and importance, and I thus implore that BEING, *whose government extends to the thoughts of all his creatures, so to direct mine*, in this arduous undertaking, that nothing hurtful to my fellow citizens may fall from my pen, and that this work may be the means of lessening a portion of some of the greatest evils of human life." And in describing the character of Dr. Sydenham, Dr. Rush declares—"I am disposed to ascribe to his sublime and just conceptions of the Deity, much of that force and extent of mind which enabled him to produce a revolution in medicine."

It is apparent that piety and religion involve an experience of emotions and feelings different from the abstract deductions of the faculties of the understanding. It is also evident that the results of the inward teaching of the Gospel, commanding also the service of the mental faculties, immeasurably transcend all that mankind had before attained. At the Christian era, the Greeks had reached the highest civilization and knowledge of any people on earth; but the Apostle Paul found them superstitiously worshipping gods "dwelling in temples made with hands." Him whom they darkly perceived and ignorantly worshipped, and to whom they had erected an altar with this inscription, "*To the Unknown God,*" he declared unto them as the "God that made the world and all things therein," and admonished them "that they should seek the Lord, if haply they might *feel after* him, and *find* him, though he be not far from every one of us." Their philosophy had given them but an obscure idea of this the "only true God," and they knew as little of "the words of eternal life," as Pilate, when he asked our Saviour, under trial before him, "What is truth?" But let the fruits determine how much the Gospel first committed to ignorant fishermen transcended the highest attainments of the most enlightened and acute philosophy the world had afforded. Socrates, the wisest and best of the Greeks, had a vague idea of an attendant spirit, but all superstitiously worshipped fancied deities represented in wood and stone; degrading practices and revolting crimes pervaded the heathen world, and their philosophy made no approach to the sublime and effective Truth as taught by Jesus, and brought home to the severest test of the highest sincerity of *feeling*. His disciples and followers were required to do unto others as they would be done unto; they were not to yield to even an imaginative impurity; and as they prayed in truthful sincerity to an all-seeing God, in the hope to be forgiven, were they to forgive all others, though enemies, their transgressions; to do good for evil; and to love even those that hated them. No merely human philosophy of man's intellect could have soared to results so sublimely pure, so authoritatively self-exacting. And it is through devotional and holy feelings, and the Divine grace and inspiration shed upon them, that such truths are alone truly and spiritually discerned, and made fruitful in their application. It is thus a witness to the truth is developed in the souls of men, answering to and appreciative of the numberless truths set forth in the Holy Scriptures, that will the most effectively set at nought all cavilling at their authenticity. Nothing can be more true than the great moral precepts and religious doctrines there recorded, as tested by all fair experience and reflection; nothing elsewhere so purifying, exalting, and redeeming from sin and corruption; nothing so satisfying and consolatory to the human soul, as the Life and Immortality of the Gospel.

The circumspection of one now commemorated, all of whose mature life was engaged in the service of an elder of the Church, admonishes me not to pass from this serious subject without the cautionary explanation required by truth and experience. While fully acknowledging the perfect purity and truthfulness of the Divine light shed upon the souls of men, Friends are fully sensible of the imperfections of human nature, and how greatly an imperfect medium of transmission may refract, tinge, and discolour the rays of ineffable brightness. The capacity to receive is limited; the range of thought is bounded; passion may disturb, interest bias, self-will mislead, superstition cloud, sin taint, and disease discolour; and that which descended in the purity of light become mixed, perverted, darkened, and lost. Of these disturbing causes, Friends have ever been and must ever be watchful; but exceptional occurrences cannot justly be seized upon by those of differing faith, to draw in question that Fountain of Light which is as essential to the moral and religious well-being of man as the sun to the physical world. Misguided zeal and wild enthusiasm may run into extravagance; or the life of religion may be lost in cold and formal observances; unauthorized prophecy may disappoint or be the unhappy cause of its own fulfilment; and disobedience lead into error and utter darkness; but the light of Truth remains for ever the same, and those who will receive it with purity of heart, and unperverted and unclouded intellect, will find in it the perfection of wisdom both to enlighten the understanding and regulate the conduct. Instead of arrogating a claim to infallibility, no Christian people are more constantly wary and apprehensive of man's inherent infirmities and liability to misapprehend, to err, or fall away from an humble dependence upon the true Guide; but the delinquencies of the erring and unfaithful cannot justly bring into question Truth itself.

In the freedom of transition required by the progress of the Memoir, I proceed to other subjects.

In the year 1825, Robert Owen, whose establishment at New Lanark, Scotland, in copartnership with William Allen, and other well-known philanthropists, gave him a favourable introduction in America, undertook to establish a pattern community in New Harmony, Indiana. Some near and dear to our parents, were induced by benevolent considerations, to join the settlement; but not without deep concern and apprehension on their part for the result. The 29th of 7 mo., 1825, P. Price writes, "The more I reflect on the subject, the more I am convinced of the delusion, and that it will end in disappointment and ruin. I am more and more convinced that the foundation is laid in the sand and it cannot stand." Just one year thereafter, in answer to a communication announcing the dissatisfaction of the parties referred to, he speaks of the result as expected, and as a system "established upon a foundation to be compared to a quicksand, that the more they built on it the deeper it would sink. It is utterly impracticable to form a community that shall unite in promoting each others' happiness, without pure Christian principles of the greatest simplicity. It is in vain to say that all Christian religious sects are in error, and therefore there must be something more substantial to build upon. Although there may be a large proportion of professors who are not strictly governed by those pure principles, yet I trust there are many endeavouring with strict integrity to follow the Captain of their salvation. The error is not in the principle, but in the conduct of those who do not submit to be governed by it. The example of the truly upright followers of a crucified Saviour, has a powerful influence on society, and generally restraining power. When I consider what would be the effect of R. O.'s opinions, were they generally adopted,—that we are the creatures of circumstances, and, therefore, cannot be accountable for our actions,—having no will of our own to do good or bad,—no governing principle of action, and, therefore, no fear of punishment for evil, or hope of reward for good actions,—I am convinced it must lead us back to a state far worse than the dark and heathen ages of the world, before the Gospel dispensation."

The concern of Rachel Price, on the same occasion, was also expressed before the result was known, substantially in these terms: "We feel a deep interest in your welfare. You claim a great portion of my thoughts and desires for your preservation, by night and by day,—the last before I close mine eyes to sleep, and the first when I awake. Often, very often, when favoured with ability, is the secret and fervent petition put up to the Preserver of men, on your accounts, that He may be pleased to keep you from evil, and turn your hearts more fully to Himself;—that you may feel for yourselves the necessity of Divine assistance,—to direct even in outward concerns. But how much more important the well-being of the immortal soul! It is not in man that walketh to direct his own steps, but the good man's ways are ordered of the Lord. This is my firm belief, from experiencing His preserving power to be near even from early life to the present time, causing great uneasiness when I went astray, and affording sweet peace for doing well. I am also from experience fully confirmed in the belief that there are in the mind two opposite spirits striving in us, the one leading to virtue and happiness, the other drawing into every kind of disorder and crime, consequently to woe and misery. Good and evil are set before us, and we must assuredly have the power of choice, and on making that choice wisely must depend our happiness in this existence and in that hereafter. How awfully important then the consideration; and may it sink deeply into our minds. If persuaded to lay aside the belief of free agency, we should, with all our boasted knowledge, reason, and philosophy, sink into mere machines to be acted upon by circumstances. I acknowledge that much may be done by precept and example, in forming the character of youth. But there is a power of choice and a free agency to elect the course of action, with a consequent accountability; and a gift of Divine grace dispensed to every individual of the human family for his preservation and everlasting happiness,—leaving him without excuse for disobedience and subject to the penalty thereof. I concur in the opinion that there is no effect without its cause; but that there is a Great First Cause of all causes is evident. All the contrivance, harmony, wisdom, and wonders of the universe proclaim His works as the creation of an all-wise, omnipotent, and omnipresent Creator.

It is the Almighty power whose law connects
The eternal chain of causes and effects;
'Tis He who made the eye and formed the listening ear,
To improve the mind by what we see and hear.

"To other animals He has given admirable instincts to guide them : 'Yea, the stork in the heaven knoweth her appointed times; and the turtle, and the crane, and the swallow, observe the time of their coming.' And to man He has given reason and understanding for his government; but, above all, to him is also given, the free gift of His Divine grace and light, as a guide through life unto salvation."

It was found out that this pattern community had truly been built upon a sandy foundation, and it sunk to rise no more. The judgments of those who had been attracted to it by delusive hopes were soon corrected by actual observation, and they returned to the bosom of general society, there to pursue their avocations for their individual profit and the aggregate advantage. They returned with a valuable lesson in human experience, the more firmly fixed in right principles, and the fervent prayers of the righteous were accomplished. It was there proved, as often before, and often may be again, that the only reliable incentive for efficient exertion for man's maintenance and improvement of his condition, is that of his own interest, by securing to himself by law the complete protection of the fruits of his own industry. This alone will secure from each individual the greatest exertion and thrift, and carry the wealth of the community to the highest aggregate amount. This is the hope of the poor man as well as of the rich, for what worthy and industrious poor man is there that does not expect himself to realize, or that his children may, property for his comfort and independence in age? There will, of course, be cases of failure to succeed, and of inevitable hardships, but for these society must provide through her taxes, or the benevolent bestow their charities for relief. The enterprise begotten by this principle of action, gives a life and energy that keeps the social body in health and prosperity,—while communities, adopting a community of property, even where they can be held together by some peculiar fanaticism or religious profession, lose the highest incentive to human effort, and comparatively stagnate, become monotonous, and tend to extinction. It is when man is left free to choose and exert his own energies, under all the varying vicissitudes of society, as it has received its cast by all time and circumstances, physical, moral, and religious, that he achieves his highest success and obtains his greatest happiness. It is only then that life has a variety that gives it spice, and presents rewards to whet the appetite of highest enterprise. The natural development of the social arrangement is into families,—these smallest communities accomplishing the greater and better part of education, government, and protection, that maintain the order and security of society; and in the domestic circle, unfolding the most pleasing attributes and affections of the human heart, delightful for all good men to contemplate, and God to behold,—for "God setteth the solitary in families."

The writer freely confesses that he at the time sympathized with the experiment at New Harmony, so far as it promised a more equal and just distribution of the products of labour, and to afford the labourer a better opportunity to rise in the scale of social improvement, and in the acquisition of wealth and influence. He yet thinks that there is a great dereliction of duty on the part of those who legislate and have power to regulate the employment of labour in this respect. Those having capital, skill, and influence, should be encouraged, by its being made their interest, to divide profits with those who labour in proportion to their successful exertion of skill and industry, and incorporated or limited partnership manufactories should be put in motion, as New England whaling vessels are sailed, for a proportionate benefit to all, thus giving to all the highest incentive for the exertion of the greatest thrift, industry, and skill. But the dividend of profit should go to the individual account, and be felt and taken as the separate resource of every separate family, whose independent existence and the sanctity of whose relations should never be broken in upon by any earthly polity.

It was in advanced life, that the severest trials that proved the faith, patience, and love of the subjects of this Memoir, awaited them. The causes that had for some years before been actively operative, brought the difficulties in the Society of Friends to a crisis at the Yearly Meeting held in Philadelphia, in 1827. These causes related to doctrines, and the administration of the disciplinary affairs of the society. The influence that practically had guided the measures of the society was in comparatively a few, though all members of adult age were admitted to its ordinary meetings for discipline. All there were at equal liberty to express their views; but only those spoke with weight whose communications carried with them the evidence of a Divine qualification and authority, and whose lives afforded the test of bearing good fruits. Such were recommended to the ministry, advanced to be elders, and appointed to superintend education, and to represent the society in a Meeting for Sufferings. These met in select meetings, and were not renewed by periodical appointments, but others were added as qualification appeared to be furnished and the service required. The frequent meetings of these select bodies afforded opportunities of a comparison of views, and naturally resulted in a concert of opinion and action. When the members of the body of the society became agitated upon the subject of doctrines and the steps taken to check the spread of those believed by many to be unsound, though thought by others to be edifying, a central influence was found to prevail in Philadelphia, and a jealousy arose through the society that this influence was operative to prejudge questions in its general meetings. Complaints were made that members were continued in the select bodies after their useful service had ceased, and after they failed truly to represent the views of those who appointed them; that the Meeting for Sufferings had attempted to impose a declaration of faith contrary to the practice of ancient Friends, who had avoided fettering the society with a creed; and that prominent members had unduly interfered with the progress in his religious service of an eminent minister, travelling under the usual sanction from another yearly meeting. With those thus complained of, the English ministers then travelling in this country concurred in sentiment, and the part they took served to awaken a further opposition by arousing the American feeling of independence and jealousy of an influence in the mother country. On the other hand, they that were designated orthodox, believed and charged that doctrines were preached and otherwise promulgated, that tended to lay waste the authority of the Holy Scriptures, to question the divinity of our Saviour, his propitiatory sacrifice for the sins of mankind and mediatorial advocacy with the Father: and believing that the vital interests of Christianity were at stake, felt justified by the extraordinary emergency in resorting to more than usual measures and in acting without the accustomed unity of the members, which had theretofore remarkably characterized the movements of the society. In fact, the bond of unity that had constituted them one society, had been broken, and a forbearing condescension and united action was not to be expected from distinct bodies, acting under repelling influences, but only that each division should look to its own conservation. The charges of unsoundness in faith by one portion against the other, were again generally denied, and a conformity with the doctrines of the founders of the society averred, and that whatever charges of unsoundness were applicable now, were only such as were made against and applicable to ancient Friends by those from whom they had been gathered to unite as a society.

Each division appealed to the writings of ancient Friends, to prove the correctness of its opinions, by the publication of numerous extracts from their writings. These were convincing to the members of each that they were standing on the true foundation, but did not reconcile those in the opposing ranks. Whatever may have been the diversity of individual opinions among primitive Friends, the cementing power that united them was now lost; and many leaders among modern Friends had not only inclined to opposing extremes of opinion left in the writings of their ancestors, but under the prevailing excitement and distrust, were mutually suspected and charged by opponents as having gone beyond the range of opinions formerly entertained. They might both, as they did, profess to believe in the doctrine of the inward light, and to support all of the invaluable testimonies of the society; but the bond of religious fellowship had been severed, their love had been replaced by distrust and repulsion of feeling, and they were no longer united by common sufferings inflicted by an intolerent and persecuting world.

Generally the minorities in the respective meetings retired from the majority, and each portion formed or kept its connexion with the yearly and subordinate meetings of discipline which it elected to join or continued to adhere to. The right of property became the subject of litigation in several of the States; but it was apparent, that even before temporal tribunals, each litigant party was quite as anxious to establish its claim to be the true Society of Friends, as to gain the property in contest. To the credit of both, however, it can be truly said that they soon wearied of litigation; the controversy was found uncongenial and distasteful, and both yielded supposed rights of great value rather than continue a strife wasteful of their spiritual well-being and Christian profession.

The difficulty with those who adhered to the Yearly Meeting of 4th month, 1827, that continued its sittings upon regular adjournments at the same place, and over to the next year, was, that apprehending those in its connexions to be the only true society, it would be an abandonment of obligatory trusts to come into any arrangement for the voluntary division of the property; while their opponents as sincerely claimed to be a portion of the Society of Friends, and to be equally within the purpose of the trusts. It was not to be expected of human nature that where so much feeling existed, such an arrangement could be consummated. The writer has no right to judge those so much better and purer than himself, yet he could not but cherish the thought that if Friends could have come to an amicable and equitable division of property, they would have set an example to the world of more value than the property to be thereby sacrificed, fitting to be recorded with the history of their leading and glorious triumphs of principle, when they treated with and paid the Indians for lands that by chartered right was already the Proprietary's; when as pioneers they secured religious toleration; and when, obedient to the calls of humanity, they enfranchised their slaves, and zealously co-operated for the abolition of the slave trade. In scriptural authority, they had before them the beautiful and persuasive example of Abraham and Lot—each willing to yield to the other the right to take to the right hand or to the left, for the enjoyment of what a bountiful Providence had amply supplied for their flocks and herds, and their households and people.

In respect to the legal right so to have adjusted the rights of property, when it is considered that it is a cherished principle of our jurisprudence to favour amicable settlements, and that family compacts made for the determination of controversy, are upheld as of sacred obligation, because they avert litigation and preserve peace, it could hardly be doubted that the tribunals of justice would meet in the same spirit and most willingly affirm the amicable treaties of divided religious associations. Can this be questioned when the Supreme Court of Pennsylvania has reiterated the recommendation that the litigant members of a divided religious society should "part in peace, having settled their claims to the property on the basis of mutual and liberal concession," and expressed the confident trust that, even in the contingency of revolution, "to the justice and forbearance of the majority of the association, whose very object is to deal justly, love mercy, and walk humbly, the minority cannot appeal in vain?" 1 W. & S. 40. But no word of censure of Friends is intended to be here implied: it is only the indulgence of the thought, perhaps an enthusiastic one, that those who have been always so self-sacrificingly just, and so prominent in the cause of humanity, might, even in this respect, have gone counter to all known practice, and transcended the example of the world.

From an early period of life Philip Price had been a member of all those select bodies of Friends of infrequent change of members. He participated in the opinion, and entertained a solemn conviction, that unsound doctrines had been preached and were making progress in the society. The Yearly Meeting to which he belonged did not provide by an amendment of the discipline to meet the extraordinary emergency, that a separation from its subordinate meetings should be accepted as a resignation, or make such act itself a cause of disownment, without the visitation and effort at reclamation which the discipline required in its usual course of administration. The task of disowning equal and often greater numbers, was left as an imperative but very onerous duty on the members, in stations requiring them to carry out the requisitions of the discipline. These visitations were regarded by the parties visited and disowned, and who recognised their own body as the true society, as useless aggravations of the existing differences and feelings; and it was not to be expected that such visits would generally be received with complacency or meekness. This unwelcome duty Philip Price performed among friends and neighbours; and also as one of a committee to visit the Southern Quarter, where but few remained in the same connexion to perform the duty. The respect and veneration felt for the man, caused him to be received with kindness, but the ordeal was the severest his kind nature had ever been subjected to, and sorrow and tears were often his portion. Yet he did his duty according to what he believed required of him, to the acquittal of his own conscience, and of his obligation to his religious society and his Creator.

A similar allotment of service did not devolve on Rachel Price. As a minister, she was not so much expected to take an active part in disciplinary duties; and as such she had felt bound to be watchful for her own preservation and usefulness; and to keep her mind and feelings disengaged from those matters of controversy which divided the members of the society. She dwelt in the Gospel love that had so much distinguished Friends in prior times, and her heart yearned towards all, that they might dwell in humility at the feet of the Saviour: and it was in the assemblies of the youth; of her own descendants; and of a few undivided meetings, that she most freely poured forth her feelings in Gospel ministration, and experienced the sweetest relief and consolation, declaring unto them, "By this shall all men know that ye are my disciples, that ye have love one for another."

The division in the society carried their children and remoter descendants into different religious associations. This was a source of deep trial to the most affectionate of parents, and to the children by whom they were beloved. They were separated in the performance of man's highest duty,—in their religious worship,—with which the domestic affections delight to commingle; yet the parental and filial attachment withstood this severest of trials. The language often repeated in her religious communications was now spoken with an especial significance and deeply impressive effect: the maternal appeal was made in the words of the Divine Master—that their fellowship should bear His test of discipleship, and that they should experimentally know that "God is Love, and he that dwelleth in love dwelleth in God, and God in him." In proportion to the laceration was this balm graciously dispensed to heal the wound. The parents' love endured with life. The filial and fraternal affection of their descendants survives the grave; and that it may survive to all when time shall be no more to them, is their fervent prayer.

In reference to the former condition of the society within her recollection, and afterwards as she saw it when torn by divisions and scattered asunder, I find the following expression of the feelings of our beloved mother; uttered not in censure of any, but in lamentation of visible results, restrictive of her own exercises in the Gospel ministry. "When I consider those days of favour to our once happy society, and compare them with the present, my mind is clothed with mourning, and according to my small measure, I can adopt the language of the prophet Joel, when he says—'Let the bridegroom go forth of his chamber, and the bride out of her closet: Let the priests, the ministers of the Lord, weep between the porch and the altar, and let them say—Spare thy people, O Lord, and give not thine heritage to reproach, that the heathen should rule over them; wherefore should they

say among the people, Where is their God?' May the Lord be jealous of His name and pity the people." * *
"Of latter times, I have felt my way very much closed from frequent communication in the exercise of my gift, or in travelling to visit friends in their meetings, from causes over which I had no control. I desire to wait in patience and resignation, endeavouring to know the Divine Will, and to do it according to my ability, having no will of my own, but leaving it to Him that hath the key of David: He that openeth and no man shutteth, and shutteth and no man rightly openeth. If it should be His will that my way should yet be closed, and my harp hung on the willow, and my tongue cleave to the roof of my mouth, yet may I remember Zion, and prefer Jerusalem above my chiefest joy. This language is often the companion of my mind—'Be still, and know that I am God.'"

Each division has since felt the value of the lesson of 1827, in its bitter consequences, and a forbearance has been exercised by each under subsequent difficulties, that if then mutually observed, it is believed, would have averted the rent of that period. Individuals might have been disowned, but the integrity of the body have been preserved. To the truth and wisdom of the following passages in the Address of the Yearly Meeting, held in the *Fourth* month, 1847, nothing can be added. "The enemy of truth and of the soul's salvation, has succeeded by various stratagems in marring the beauty and peace of Zion, and it behooves all those who are desirous of seeing the waste places built up, and the former paths restored, to put shoulder to shoulder, and walking by the same rule, and minding the same thing, rally to *first principles,* and labour harmoniously in the great work of our duty." "Against these dangers which threaten the Church, there is but one defence,—a hearty and practical return to First Principles. The light of Christ which shineth in every man, which is the swift reprover of sin, and shines more and more in the humble and obedient soul, unto the perpect day, will, if we follow its guidance in all things as it makes them manifest, lead us into all truth and unto all humility and holiness." "This humble, consistent walking, a godly zeal, the love of each other in that fellowship which is in the ever-blessed and unchangeable Truth, would again distinguish us as a people, and it would again be said of us as of old, 'See, how these Quakers love one another!'"

The "Appeal for the Ancient Doctrines of Friends," from which the preceding extracts are made, was prepared and issued by those who had twenty years before combated what they believed to be errors of heretical tendency, but now, turning to the other extreme of the doctrinal platform, exerted the same ability and research to exculpate the Society of Friends from the imputation of opinions nearly allied to those of the churches from which ancient Friends had separated. Thus prepared with the care and wariness induced by the recollection of the recent history of the society on the one hand, and, on the other, in refutation of writings assimilated in doctrine to the views of the persecutors of the founders of their religious community, the "Appeal" is based in neither extreme, and is a close and careful exposition of the doctrines of the society, distinctly recognising "the more sure word of prophecy" to be "the *Word* nigh in the heart"—from which the Scriptures came, and in and by which the Scriptures are to be interpreted.

It becomes the writer to speak with the greatest diffidence upon the subject of doctrines, but he would be derelict to the duty he has ventured to assume, were he to leave unstated a summary of the faith of his parents. Their faith was Orthodox, in the sense that the Society of Friends had always been orthodox. Theirs was not a dead faith, unproductive of good works. It was a faith, believing in the authenticity and Divine authority of the Holy Scriptures, but understanding them with the light of the Holy Spirit that inspired their penmen; a faith believing in the "miraculous conception, birth, miracles, doctrines, crucifixion, and resurrection of our Lord and Saviour Jesus Christ;"* but ever waiting on His spiritual appearance in the heart, who "brought life and immortality to light;" a faith believing in a reconciliation, for-

* Letter of P. Price.

giveness, and justification through Him, but to be preceded by a repentance of sin, a regeneration and sanctification of the soul,—a being justified because made just by the operations and a submission to His Holy Spirit, without which, all human efforts, in worship, in prayer, and in sanctification, would be vain and unavailing; and believing, that without such repentance and justification, in the final judgment man will be adjudged according to the deeds done in the body.

Friends, in all times, since they rose, have endured the charge of heterodoxy from sects claiming to be orthodox. The ground of the charge has mainly been that Friends have preferred to adhere to the Spirit of the Scriptures of Truth, as they find them to have been written; refusing, therefore, to adopt unscriptural terms and deductions made from them in man's will and wisdom. They have preferred that the evidences of their faith should be found in a life of righteousness, in their obedience to the spiritual appearances of our Saviour and to His commandments left while on earth, wherein each individual must experience the work of his own regeneration, redemption, and salvation to be wrought in his own soul. "For the grace of God that bringeth salvation hath appeared to all men, teaching us, that, denying ungodliness and worldly lusts, we should live soberly, righteously, and godly, in this present world." Instead of falling short of others, true Quakerism is religion's power in its highest efficacy—is sincere, self-sacrificing, earnest, and devoted, in love to God and love to man—a fervent belief in Him whom to believe in is "everlasting life"—the Messiah, the Lord and Saviour Jesus Christ.

Many others than members have lamented events so keenly deplored by the subjects of this Memoir, and by all who have been faithfully concerned for the welfare of the Church. The conservative example for all that regarded good order and sound principle, and the unceasing philanthropical labours of Friends, had ever been of salutary and pervading influence, and it was a source of regret to all who could appreciate their virtues, that they should be in any degree shorn of their power of usefulness. Their mutual love and fraternal aid were a marvel to others, and while their charity to their own poor is so much unseen as to be little known, their affluence of love and charity have also unceasingly flowed to others beyond the pale of their society. It is true they ever warn their youth to abstain from the vain fashions and seductive allurements of the world, and to keep up the hedging of a distinctive dress and language, but when proved and fortified by experience, their humane and gifted emissaries, clothed with the armour of Christ, have ever been obedient to the calls of humanity, and maintained the Christian warfare for the reformation of mankind—of the action of mind upon mind, of feeling upon feeling, and of the principle of truth over error, and of goodness over evil. To the well-wishers of human progress and improvement, whether within or without the society, therefore, it was cause of mourning that the spirit of discord could find entrance into such a fraternity of love and peace—that so beautiful a temple of harmonious proportion as this living Church, could have been riven to its foundation. But it was those who had long enjoyed the spiritual benefits and happiness of the religious association that most keenly felt the lacerations of broken ties and alienated friendships—mournfully beheld their waste places, and, in the bitterness of sorrow, heard the songs of Zion as in exile from brethren and the spiritual homes where they had worshipped together.

Were it permitted of one who can claim no influence to utter a prayerful wish, it would be that the blessed Power who is ever operative to restore the disturbed equilibriums of His natural creation, who beneficently heals the wounded, "binds up the broken-hearted," and is ever shedding the light of His glorious Truth, should continue to allay all unhappy feelings, and as His holy love shall draw His people to Himself, He will ever draw them into a Gospel fellowship and unity with each other, and though they should not worship together, and "neither in this mountain, nor yet in Jerusalem, worship the Father,"—yet may they worship Him in the same spirit and in the same truth and faith. And may they never forget the value of those testimonies of truth and humanity which their common religious ancestors upheld and established under the sharpest persecutions, and that the righteous principles they cherished were dearer to them than property or life; that the history of their descendants, as theirs, may, as the course of a pure and beneficent stream, brightly contrast with the dark and crimsoned annals of mankind, and reflect the glory of Him that is the fountain of all light.

During the summer of 1833, Philip and Rachel Price visited together many of their friends and relatives in Maryland, and parts of Pennsylvania, in going and returning. The occasion seems to have been social, rather than a religious service. Returning, they visited and were welcomed by their venerable friends William and Hannah Jackson. The former, then in his eighty-first year, had from infirmity ceased to attend meetings of worship, but his mind was bright, filled with love, and wakeful to the condition of the religious world. On its being remarked to him that it was an inexpressible favour, when the body was afflicted so as to prevent attendance at places of Divine worship, to know "that He whom we meet to worship is not confined to temples made with hands, but continues to condescend to meet with those who sincerely seek Him, even in their lonely habitations;" William replied, "Yes,—my love is towards them,—and in all our weakness of body and mind, He permits us to feel and know that we are not forsaken, by the frequent incomes of Divine love in our hearts, whereby the mind is strengthened to hold on in its way, bearing in remembrance that here we have no continuing city, and that our generation must pass and another arise." He expressed for himself an entire resignation and willingness to pass away. He referred with a lively interest to the rise of the society, and made a comparison between the present and the times of George Fox, when there was great commotion and unsettlement about religion, and the different sects contended for supremacy. But these "did not sufficiently consider that an outward profession of faith, however good, without the experimental knowledge of the operation of the Divine Spirit on the secret heart, is not sufficient for our purification, justification, or redemption. Things being in this state, George Fox invited the people to Christ within, the hope of glory, the true light which lightens every man. As they gathered to this, as the standard of light and life, and settled under its operations in the heart, withdrawing from outward ceremonies and forms, there was a great revival of true religion. I have believed, on weighing the subject, that if the people in this land, and in this our day and time of commotion, would centre down in their minds to the same Divine principle in the heart, there would be again a gathering to the Light, and the knowledge of the Lord would increase a thousand fold, and as faithfulness should be kept to, the reign of the

Prince of Peace would more and more abound." The narrator, Rachel Price, adds, "I cannot convey the feelings of my own mind more fully than by saying they have long been in accordance with what he expressed in the interesting interview we had with him."

The Society of Friends, from the settlement of the province of Pennsylvania by William Penn, following his good example of kindness and justice, in a spirit of grateful humanity, has ever maintained friendly relations with the Indian tribes, and its members have devoted much time and means for their improvement in the arts of civilized life, and their moral and religious instruction. When more contiguous, the care of the society was more immediate and constant, begetting frequent interviews, and councils together, and addresses full of interest and instruction. For these injured and expelled sons of the forest, the sympathies of Rachel Price were always intensely awake. The records of the councils held with Friends and Deputy Governors, speeches delivered, &c., were procured and copied by her own hand. When the Cherokees published a newspaper, it was subscribed for, read, and contributed to, by her. She wrote to encourage them in the worship of the "Great Spirit,"—the "Common Father" of all,—to abstain from the use of ardent spirits,—from holding slaves,—holding up to their view, that "Surely the God of mercy and justice will one day or other plead the cause of the oppressed African, as well as that of the afflicted Indian; He who of one blood created all nations on the earth,—who is our common Father,—who has in his Divine goodness and mercy granted a portion of his Holy Spirit, as a witness placed in each of our hearts."

When that tribe was required by the policy of the General Government to remove to the west, she felt bound to raise her voice, though that of a feeble woman, in a feeling, pathetic, and solemn remonstrance, addressed to the President of the United States, pleading with him for the Indian, as she had with the Indian for the African. To be sure no result was likely to come from the appeal, but it was uttered in that authority that she was not at liberty to disobey. Quoting the Great Commandment of our Saviour, "that whatsoever ye would that men should do unto you, do ye even so to them," reciting the obligations of treaties formed, the example of Penn, and the duty of kindness and protection to the original owners of the soil, she proceeded to say, "The sympathetic feelings in the minds of many of the people are very much awakened on behalf of the natives remaining within the limits of some of the southern states, whose rulers seem determined to dispossess them, and drive them from the land of their forefathers, and from their comfortable homes,—made so by their own industry and economy, under the encouragement of former administrations of our government." "Permit a feeble female voice to plead for that distressed, afflicted people,—for sixty thousand individuals, equally the objects of redeeming love and mercy with ourselves, who profess the sacred name of Christians." "We deeply feel for our beloved country, lest by any rash or cruel act upon the helpless, the Almighty Power may see meet to avenge their wrongs. Although He is a God of mercy, He is also a God of justice, and will recompense us according to our works. 'For the crying of the poor and the sighing He will arise.' May the prayers of the sincere of heart be availing with Him who can turn the heart of man, and cause him to know that the Most High ruleth in the kingdoms of men. 'It is shewn unto thee, oh man, what is good, and what the Lord thy God hath required of thee,—to deal justly, to love mercy, and walk humbly before thy God.' If man, presuming in his own strength and power, persists in his own will to raise the iron hand of oppression, to exterminate the unoffending and helpless, may we not fear that He that hath all power in heaven and on earth, may see meet to turn it on the head of the oppressor?" "May the President of the United States be willing to pause and reflect, remembering that 'not the hearers are just before God, but the doers of the Law shall be justified.'" "We are both advanced in life, and the time fast approaching when the awful language may be sounded in our ears, 'Steward, give up thy stewardship, for thou mayst be no longer steward.' May the King of kings, and Lord of lords, who is God over all the families of the earth, incline thy heart to justice, truth, and mercy."

In behalf of the Indians, in answer to the allegation against them that "civilization must displace barbarism"—she advocated, in their Gazette, their right to remain on the footing of their advanced civilization. "Is not this realized in and by the Cherokee nation and several other tribes? It would no doubt spread far and wide under the protecting care of a kind Providence, encouraged by a mild, pacific government,—like that of our worthy predecessor (William Penn), or under the fatherly, fostering protection of such a President as George Washington. Notwithstanding you may be driven from the land of your forefathers by the powerful hand of man, even beyond the Rocky Mountains, remember that you cannot go beyond the care of Him who regards even the sparrows, of Him who said to his disciples, 'are not ye of more value than many sparrows?' "

In the year 1836, our beloved parents made their last journey together, to visit their daughter in Susquehanna county, on the north border of Pennsylvania, and other friends in the state of New York. Our mother made some notes of impressions on this journey, and it is interesting to observe the effects of new objects upon her reflective mind. It was probably her first ride by steam power, and she could not but regard the locomotive with its fire and puffing, whisking its long train along, as having "an infernal appearance," and its rapid motion, like flying through the air from time to eternity. The slower pace in the canal boat up the Susquehanna, permitted time for observation and reflection, in better keeping with her own feelings. "We passed moderately along at the rate of four miles an hour, which afforded us an opportunity of looking upon the scenery; the works of art and the sublime works of the Creator; the lofty mountains and the rocks hanging over the river,—the beautiful flowers of various kinds, all adding to the grandeur or loveliness of the scene, and producing a sweet sensation, comparable to the calm decline of life, when the day's work seems to be almost done. There was one subject of reflection which occurred often in our travelling, particularly on the rivers and mountains, striking my mind with great force, particularly in passing up the Susquehanna,—that all these romantic scenes had been from time immemorial in the possession of the Indians,—their peaceful homes,—their hunting grounds,—their fisheries; where were their wigwams, and all the comforts they required in their wandering manner of life. But now, they are driven off by the whites from these abodes, designed no doubt by our Great Benefactor for their benefit as well as ours,—a poor and oppressed people, permitted now to have no share of what was justly their own. In solemn retrospect, the hillocks I see appear to my imagination as the graves of the nations that have passed away!"

Her notes mention their cordial reception by their warm friend, Charles Miner, near Wilkesbarre, and speak of a visit with him to the Baltimore mine of coal, but not of the impressions and remarks there made, which much interested his mind. To one who had never seen such an excavation into the interior of the earth, between massive jet columns of coal, supporting at great height a roof of slate, that itself sustained the incumbent hill, the impression made was grand and imposing, and not unmingled with emotions of astonishment at the boldness of man, in thus venturing to penetrate and disturb the bowels of the earth—but was quickly followed by the grateful acknowledgments to an all-wise and bountiful Creator, who had thus treasured up in ages long past, this resource of fuel and comfort for the present and future generations of men.

But a recent letter from the pen of her attentive conductor, gives more of the details of this visit to the mine: "When we came in full view of those lofty pillars and vast caverns, seemingly dark from the contrast with the glare of day in which we stood, she paused, and her eye passed over the scene in a deliberate survey. Presently she began with much cheerfulness to observe and to inquire. The unmistakeable traces of vegetable impressions, and even of the roots and stumps of large trees in the slate-rocks, were objects of special notice and examined with delighted curiosity; a few for their own beauty, but chiefly as they impressed her mind with their great antiquity; and especially as furnishing strong proof that coal was not a mineral but of vegetable origin. We rather waited her pleasure to move, than led the way to enter the mine. Her inquiries, remarks, cheerfulness, and evident enjoyment, were a source of pleasure to us all. After examining the various layers or seams of coal apparent in the pillars, differing in thickness and quality, and divided by their lamina of slate; and listening to the suggestion that they indicated that the whole body of coal was not formed at one time, but by successive layers, and at long intervals, I ventured to speak of the pecuniary value of the mine, showing the results by cubic yards and per acre, to be very great. She smiled, but made no reply. Having completed the exploration, we returned near to the place of entrance and paused, the mind of your excellent mother apparently absorbed in thought. A deep feeling of solemnity seemed to come over us all. After a few minutes' silence, she spoke to this effect: 'The visit to this place has been to me a source of rational pleasure and desirable information. In it are combined, in a wonderful degree, the beautiful and instructive, from objects of minute examination unto the sublime in rude magnificence and vastness. I cannot conceive that an intelligent and rightly disposed mind could behold what we have seen to-day without its awakening a very solemn train of reflections. I am sensible these mines give profitable employment to many labourers, and thus render many families comfortable, and am aware of their great commercial value; but my mind has been led to consider them in a light less worldly, but not less worthy of our regard. These cold but fruitful northern latitudes seem in the future destined to be the residence of a numerous population; but food and raiment are not alone sufficient; fuel is indispensable to their comfort, if not to their existence. Hence the deposits of these inexhaustible supplies of indestructible fuel, in positions where so much is needed, are to my mind additional demonstrations of the wisdom and goodness of our beneficent Creator; and that we, his children, are the objects of his constant care. Cherishing these reflections must awaken in every breast renewed feelings of gratitude to the Divine Spirit, and of praise and thanksgiving to His Holy Name.' The outline is here, my dear friend, but to pretend to verbal accuracy would be presuming. The latter part of her remarks were more full, very pleasing, and very solemn. That they were deeply impressive on my mind you are aware—*more so than any discourse I ever heard.* I give you the rose-tree, but neither the fragrance nor the flowers."

Continuing their journey, they were pleased with the lakes and scenery in the interior of New York, and of the

North River, on the return; met a variety of company, and had new ideas to form of persons and things; "and in every situation found some congenial minds with whom we could mingle in conversation and unite in feeling." It was felt that it might be, as it proved, their last journey on earth; and it is added, "We were often reminded of the great and final journey from which no traveller will return, to the city where nothing that is impure can enter. How awful, and oh, what need there is to remember the injunction, 'watch and pray, and that continually, lest ye enter into temptation;' but the consoling promise is that 'in every nation, kindred, tongue, and people, they that fear God, and work righteousness, shall be accepted of Him.' Such is His universal love to mankind, that 'all that will come may come, and partake of the waters of life freely, without money and without price.'"

In their deportment towards their children and government of all under their authority, there was no austerity. The love and respect that all bore for them, and the fear of wounding their feelings, were sufficient restraints against disobedience. The young were encouraged by kindness to seek their presence and confide in them. The society of youth was congenial to their feelings, and the social meetings of their numerous relatives, and the friends of their children, under the paternal roof, were of frequent repetition, and the occasion of both enjoyment and instruction. There they often gathered their descendants, numbering, before the death of either, over fifty individuals, besides the husbands or wives of their ten children, who also were all received within the family circle with the same cordial affection as their own children. In that beautiful scene and hospitable mansion, to which the "untravelled hearts" of their children constantly return, as to the brightest spot and dearest home of earth, did they often collect their flock, and in the social gathering they never failed spiritually to obey the Divine injunction, "feed my lambs." The last occasion, during their lives, of a general assemblage of this description was in 1834, the fiftieth year of their marriage, at their former homestead and natal home of their children. Here, where their son-in-law and daughter maintained the ancient hospitality, met the descendants of all ages from infancy to past middle life, and after the usual entertainment, gathered in stillness and silence. It was felt to be the last occasion when so many of us would ever convene, and that the patriarchal parents could not long survive. These considerations awakened the natural sensibilities of parents and children; but greater was the paternal solicitude then expressed that their descendants should obey the Divine and inward guide, live in righteousness, and continue in that harmony and love with each other, which had ever through life been to them the cause of heartfelt thankfulness; and remembering that the old must die, the young may die, and the middle-aged do die—to prepare for the final accountability, that all might meet again in happiness, no one missing from the joyful assemblage. They had in all things endeavoured to fulfil their duties to their offspring,—to instil into their minds the precepts of justice to man, and the cheering hopes of Christian salvation,—and as they had striven to perform their duties, their earnest supplications were raised that their children should in like manner endeavour to perform their duty to their offspring,—that goodness, justice, harmony, and religious faith might flow as a stream through the succession of generations.

On the 12th day of the 2d month, 1837, Philip Price was attacked with pleurisy, which, increasing in violence, produced intense suffering, in breaking down a naturally strong constitution. His children, relatives, and friends, were allowed free admission to the sick chamber, he desiring their presence, saying in the words of Addison, that he wished them to "see in what peace a Christian can die." They sat in quietness with him during a sickness prolonged through two weeks, deeply sympathizing with the sufferer, and instructed by his patience and expressions. They truly felt that

> "The chamber where the good man meets his fate,
> Is privileged beyond the common walk
> Of virtuous life, quite in the verge of Heaven."

In the early part of the illness, the suffering was so intense, he feared that with the desire for bodily relief, he could not keep the patience. He had full confidence in the Divine Power, but felt stripped of the evidences of His presence. His beloved companion was led to recall to his recollection the situation and language of the Divine Master, while on the cross, when He was buffeted, ignominiously treated, and felt forsaken; and the pathetic language then used by the dear Redeemer, "My God, my God, why hast thou forsaken me;" that it was not for His own state that He was thus baptised, but for the sins of the whole world; thus setting an example of submission and patience to His Father's will, under the severest trials; and she fully believed that if he likewise dwelt in a measure of the same patience he would yet have to praise and testify of the Lord's goodness and mercy to his soul; and this language of encouragement brought to him consolation in his continued great bodily sufferings. He regarded this as his last illness, felt a submission to his approaching end, and that the way was clear before him. He felt at peace with all mankind, knew not that he had an enemy in the world, that he had done all in his power to assist others, had done what he could to educate his children, but had not been concerned to lay up much riches for them. The quietude of the hushed household of scholars was grateful to his feelings; they seemed, he said, to learn of one another to be kind, respectful, and considerate. Little children were called to receive the parting kiss, with the expression that even they might remember the event; and he desired that they should not only be taught useful learning, but instructed in things of a substantial, divine nature. As those relatives and friends visited him who had leaned on him for protection and kindness, his regret seemed keenest; that he must leave them now to love and help one another. He admonished all not to defer the work of preparation for the scene they were now witnessing. It was then "a poor time to lay up treasure in Heaven. Too many were deferring it to a bed of sickness; but it should be an every-day work of the whole life, and that all business should be pursued with the affections placed on high, and the world beneath our feet. On the entrance of that beloved minister of the Gospel, Sarah Emlen, he said, "*Thou* knowest how faithfully I have endeavoured to follow in the footsteps of the Divine Master, devoting my life and best ability to His service;" and received the reply, "Well do I know it and can testify to it, and I trust thou wilt be abundantly rewarded for thy submission to the Divine requisitions of our Holy Saviour." Addressing his beloved wife, he said, "We have been united in the bonds of endeared affection for more than fifty years, and now we are about to suffer a final separation on earth. I have consolation in believing that we have endeavoured to instil into the minds of our children the spirit of love, and have set such an example before them as in some degree to be effectual, and desired that this feeling should continue among them." "We have had many bitter cups through life together, but nothing to be compared with the rejoicings we have had."

As his sickness continued, aud his end approached, a sweeter peace, a firmer confidence, and a brighter hope, dawned upon the sufferer. "I could not have thought the way could be made so clear. For some days I have felt my close to be near. I know not why it is—it is no merit of my own that death is not appalling. It is admirable mercy! It is adorable goodness! It is adorable goodness! I hope I am not deceived; but I could not feel this peace, were I not enabled to trust in His armour, whom I have endeavoured to serve all my life long. The longest life is almost too short to prepare for eternity." "'Eye hath not seen, nor ear heard, neither hath it entered into the heart of man, to conceive the good things that the Lord hath in store for those who love Him.'" "The natural eye can have no perception of the splendour of the New Jerusalem; no outward representation can give an idea of it." "The Divine Wisdom, it is all sufficient; oh, do attend to it, the uncreated Word from eternity." "Verily, there is a reward for the righteous." "How short is the space from earth to Heaven! It seems but a step." On First-day, the 26th of the 2d month, much relieved of bodily pain, he gradually sank away, and with the close of the day, departed in that holy quiet, he had so much enjoyed, surrounded by his beloved wife, children, relatives and friends; his last request, "that they might partake of a holy quiet"—and in that quiet his precious soul took its flight from time to eternity; and after a solemn and prolonged pause, that awful stillness was broken by the sweet tones of one whose voice had ever called her children to a "holy quiet" and everlasting peace. Then most impressively were they made to feel, and ever will remember, that at the death of the righteous,

> "A *holy quiet* reigns around,
>   A calm which life nor death destroys;
> Nothing disturbs that peace profound,
>   Which his unfettered soul enjoys."

And there did they witness and verify the injunction to "Mark the perfect man, and behold the upright, for the end of that man is peace."

At a subsequent period, his bereft partner, adverting to this interesting scene, said, "Many of his dear descendants and friends were seated round his bed in solemn silence, and were permitted to partake of that holy quiet, and to witness the calm resignation of his mind; my soul bearing him company through the shades of death, to the happy mansions of eternal bliss;" and as a soul there welcomed "among saints and angels, and the spirits of the just made perfect," did she afterwards seem to behold him as with the perception of actual vision.

The voice of sorrow and sympathy came from many sources, but from none more sweetly than from the gifted pen of one of kindred feelings, appreciative of the like qualities and character, in the following letter, and in an obituary furnished the Wyoming Herald.

"Retreat, March 4th, 1837.

"MY DEAR FRIEND,—Your lines, in the sweet words of Ossian, were 'pleasant, but mournful to the soul.' To have been remembered and kindly spoken of, by your beloved father, our most excellent friend, in his dying hour, was an affecting, but pleasing proof of his affection for us. He always showed to us the consideration of a parent. The early friendship of your father and mother—they seemingly adopting us into their family—was not only a source of social gratification, but, from their standing in society, it was a passport to public respect and favour, of the greatest value to us, and was entitled to our most grateful acknowledgment. In a long intercourse with the world, I have never met with a man who united in himself so many claims to esteem and love. His aspect was so benignant, his manner and address were so mild and engaging, that the bosom seemed to open to him in confidence before he spoke. Then, his clear mind, sound understanding, and benevolent heart, commanded respect, inspired confidence, and enabled him to do so much good among his fellow-men. Pardon me, I could not say less, though this may not be the proper place. It is impossible not to mourn the loss of so good a man. But we are not without sources of consolation,—his sufferings are ended, and his gain infinite. He had performed his part in his day and generation most usefully and most worthily; and while performing his duty, through a long life, he has duly estimated the bounties of Providence, and rationally enjoyed them. Passed the age allotted to man,—full of Christian hope and Christian charity,—his spirit returns to his Maker, amid the tears and prayers and blessings of all who knew him. Who can say that such is not a most enviable lot? May his children emulate his virtues, and like him be useful, beloved, and happy, to as advanced an age. Lætitia joins with me in expression of sympathy and condolence to your good mother. We shall never forget her affectionate address to us when our dear Ann was taken away. Our kindest and most respectful love waits upon her, and our best regards to yourself and all the family.

From your sincere friend,

"CHARLES MINER.

"To ELI K. PRICE."

"Died, recently, at West Chester, Chester county, PHILIP PRICE, aged 74 years. Friendship would claim space in your paper, Mr. Editor, to say a word of the departed: He gained no laurels in the bloody field of battle; the clangor of the trumpet and the rolling of the drum awakened no sympathetic stirrings in his pure and chastened breast. A member of the Society of Friends, whose distinguished doctrinal tenets are derived from the character and precepts of our Saviour—to love mercy—walk humbly—not return evil for evil—when reviled to revile not again,—he bore testimony before the world that the terrible scourge of war should be done away, and man cease to butcher his fellow-man. I come to tell of no lucrative civil offices he filled. His heart never gave way to the proud aspirations of ambition, though he cherished a proper regard for those who faithfully served their country. Then what can you tell us? I can tell you, and record with sincerity and truth, a brief sketch of one of the worthiest men this generation has known.

"Philip Price was descended from a very respectable Welsh family, among the earliest settlers in Chester county. In person he was tall, well formed, of excellent though not robust constitution. His countenance mild, intelligent, and pleasing, his movements dignified and easy, and his manners and address remarkably bland and prepossessing. The mind of Mr. Price was well informed, his judgment clear and strong, united to an intuitive perception of character, and a ready apprehension of the right and proper in all matters of business. Though seeking no distinction in the walks of public life, it was impossible but such a man should have extensive influence in society. He had. And as duty led him, it was his pride (if that word may be used in connexion with his name) and pleasure to exert that influence for the benefit of his fellow-men.

"Mr. Price was among the earliest, most liberal, and enlightened of those who broke in on the old exhausting method of farming; and took the lead in introducing plaster, clover, lime, and a proper rotation of crops, the four grand pillars of improvement that have raised and sustain Chester county as one of the most rich and productive districts in Pennsylvania. No one had more influence in the excellent society of which he was a member; because that influence was ever exercised wisely and prudently, in doing good. On an eminence, in a most romantic situation, overlooking the fertile hills and rich meadows along the Brandywine, his mansion was situated, fronting to the east and south; on this elevation, his spirit seemed pure as the air he breathed; his mind appeared to expand with his expanded view, and his spirit was bright as beams of morning sun. Friendly and hospitable, it was delightful to visit there and share in the converse of himself and his amiable and intelligent partner. After educating his children with care, and seeing all of them happily settled, and most of them near him, Mr. and Mrs. Price, impressed with its great importance, and taking a parental and lively interest in the improvement of the rising generation, accepted the situation of Superintendents of West-Town School, where they remained for several years.

" Here, viewing the matter more closely, and actuated by the most pure and philanthropic motives, they formed the design to erect a School for Girls—somewhat varying and enlarging the scope and plan existing at West-Town; not in rivalship or interference with that valuable seminary; but opening their Halls to many who could not, by the rules, be admitted there. A large building, admirably adapted to the purpose, plain, simple, yet neat and commodious, now adorns the flourishing village of West Chester; while the full rooms of happy faces, and the press for admittance, show that the West Chester Boarding School for Girls, established by Philip and Rachel Price, has accomplished and is accomplishing its high and benevolent purpose. By the simple rule of that unostentatious society, no marble monument will be erected over the remains of our departed friend; but while the West Chester Boarding School for Girls shall last and flourish—and may it be perpetual—there will be a monument to the worth of Philip Price more honourable than Blenheim to its first titled possessor.

" At the age of 74, having spent a life of usefulness and virtuous enjoyment—for there never lived a happier man—surrounded by children and friends, amid the prayers and blessings of all who knew him, the good man, like the sun in a mild summer evening, full of Christian faith and Christian hope, lost to our sight but not extinguished, sinks calmly and sweetly to rest."

Rachel Price survived her husband more than ten years. She lived to cherish his memory, enforce his example, and enjoy the affections of her children, relatives, and friends. She was especially the object of the personal care of that daughter, who had for many years been resident with and the comfort and solace of her parents, whose father bore, as his last testimony of her, that "We are of one heart and of one mind;" whom all the other children considered as their representative in that precious and sacred charge. In the blended narrative the history of Philip and Rachel Price has been told in their principal outlines. In a more limited sphere, in her own meeting, in those near home, and in her daughter's school, the same earnest and pathetic appeals in Gospel love continued to be made by the survivor unto the end.

A few extracts from a letter written to absent sons, in 1839, will show the continued occupation and concern of her mind. "I have much to be thankful for. I am still able to get to meetings, to visit the afflicted, and my children in the neighbourhood, which I consider a great favour; and also to experience that love in my heart to increase, which binds together in the bonds of life and love. May we all know a partaking thereof, and obey the command of our Redeemer, given to his immediate followers, that we love one another, for 'by this shall all men know ye are my disciples, if ye love one another.'" * * "I am solicitous that for the short time I may yet have to remain, I may be enabled to fulfil my duty towards you; yea, to double my diligence, craving Divine aid therein, and I recommend to all of you who have tender plants committed to your care, to endeavour to guard and protect them from the many defilements of this vain world, and the besetments of the enemy of our souls' happiness; who is seeking to draw our minds off the watch, and encumbering them with the cares of the world. I know by experience that there is a great care necessary for those who have large families to provide for, to guard against the unlawful love of lawful things; and the language is, 'Seek ye first the kingdom of God and his righteousness, and all these things shall be added unto you, for your Heavenly Father knoweth that ye have need of these things.' Let us endeavour to be in readiness when the solemn inquiry may be made, 'What have you done with the lambs committed to your care in the wilderness of this world?' May we not have to answer that while we were busy, hither and thither, they made their escape." "Men that are engaged in public business are often exposed and in danger of being drawn into party feeling in politics, whereby the mind may be much engrossed, if there be not a strict watch maintained; but I do hope a word to the wise is sufficient to induce a renewed care upon this subject, as coming from the heart of an affectionate mother, whose petitions are often put up, in sincerity and truth, on behalf of herself and endeared offspring."

In the last week of her life, a son, then visiting her, writes to his distant sister: "It is very gratifying to find that with the infirmity of disease and great age upon her, our dear mother retains a clear mind, and the dispositions and affections that have characterized her through life. None of the irritation and fretfulness that is so frequently incident to such age and sickness is perceived. On the contrary, like our father, she regrets her inability to help herself, and expresses a grateful feeling for all the attentions she receives. There is a quiet dignity that will probably remain with her, however much she may be enfeebled by the further progress of disease and age. Love to all mankind abounds with her, and this love and the religious sentiments with which she has been so thoroughly imbued through life, remain with her, as part of her nature, only to cease their manifestations with the extinction of life. Many are the scriptural expressions she continues to repeat to us, with the same sweetness she has ever uttered them from the gallery and in the family circle, on serious occasions. These are now additionally impressive, as they may be the last, and are sanctioned and sanctified as if they were, as she expects not to be long with us. She has not strength to enlarge in her remarks, but from time to time repeats those truths which abide with her,—expressions and promises which are not only her own reliance and source of comfort in the extremity of life, but which she wishes to impress upon her children as their reliance and as their hope for the future;—'Come unto me, all ye that labour and are heavy laden, and I will give you rest.' 'Take my yoke upon you, and learn of me; for I am meek and lowly of heart, and ye shall find rest unto your souls.' 'Christ's invitation is for all to come unto him; I will give unto him that is athirst of the waters of life freely,' &c. The great end and purpose of religious faith she summed up in this: 'To *know* Thee, the only true God, and Jesus Christ whom thou hast sent, this is Life Eternal;' and her last charge to that son was, 'Keep a guarded care over all those placed under thy authority. *Be obedient unto the law written in the heart; and endeavour to draw others unto it; in this you will find your present and everlasting peace.*'" A few days after, when expecting her close, he wrote, "I am sad and sorrowful; yet my reflection teaches me I should be otherwise. Our mother has reached a great age, and a continuance of life would be a burthen to the spirit. Her long life has been one uniform and beautiful example, and at fourscore and four years of age, the intellect is bright; to the last her heart has remained full of love and affection to all of human kind. Through nearly a whole century, she has in simplicity and truthfulness preached the precepts of Jesus, and she departs without a blemish or a shade upon her character or intellect. If the Gospel truths she preached were few and simple, their influence was constantly present, and imparted their own serious and sublime simplicity to her character. These deeply felt and sincerely believed, with a constant hope beyond this life, she seemed never to suffer vacillation from doubts or natural propensities, in conflict with the holy influences that dwelt on her mind. Is it not then a cause of gratitude that the close should be bright, and that, almost without pain, her spirit should be released from its mortal tenement? Surely it is; and when her memory shall be all that is left of her to us, it will be most pleasing in all the residue of our lives to reflect that she lived so long and so well, and was gathered as the ripe corn, that felt not the sickle that severed it from its earthly connexion." On the evening of the same day, the 6th day of the 8th month, 1847, he further wrote, "Our beloved mother has departed this life. It is now a solemn certainty that we have heard her sweet voice for the last time; that we shall see her living countenance no more,—so divinely good. If the good recognise each other in the future world, then have the blessed spirits of our beloved parents met this day in joy, and felt the felicity that they were united in an endless bliss. This was our dear mother's fervent hope, expressed for herself and beloved offspring.

May her hope and prayer be realized, no one missing to mar the heavenly joy."

Appropriately was it asked at the last solemn gathering, when the remains of those who so loved in life were placed together in their last resting-place,

> "Oh grave! where is thy victory?
> Oh death! where is thy sting?"

At Birmingham, their earthly remains repose. There they tranquilly sleep beneath the soil once trod by hostile feet; on the spot where the battle was fought, and foe met foe in deadly strife. It was the scene of their peaceful mission. There they preached peace on earth and good will toward men. Thence are seen the hills of Brandywine, the stream that gave name to the battle, clothed with the verdure that sprung beneath their culture. The demon of war has fled,—the trace of the battle has gone,—the spirit of peace rests on the scene,—and as often as the returning seasons shall bring life and beauty to these hills and vales, will they freshly bring to mind the memory of these benefactors. No monument marks their grave; no epitaph speaks on their tomb; but the vernal bloom of these hills is a living testimony of their peaceful deeds. No lettered marble can speak their praise; but their name, their worth, their memory, are written on the tablets of living hearts; hearts, wherever they are, hither turning in affection, will, in their faith and hope and love, soar to the view of the blissful re-union of souls in a Heavenly mansion.

In all the relations of life, Philip and Rachel Price were consistent with the professions they made before the world. They were mild in temper, of equable disposition, and exempt from the irritability and eccentricity of character that often impair the dignity and usefulness of those of more active imagination and brilliant genius, and consequently more practically useful and more generally beloved. They were friendly and social with their neighbours, rendering aid in times of need, visiting the sick and the house of mourning. They had differences with none, were pacificators among others, and lived and died without an enemy. To say that in all his transactions Philip Price was governed by a strict integrity, would be short of what the truth requires. His disposition to oblige seemed not to be less than that of one who loved his neighbour as himself, and his property, his money, and his credit, were lent according to his ability, and if erring, it was on the side of excess of liberality. In aiding the progress of travelling Friends, and in their entertainment, and in providing travelling accommodations for relatives, to reach their meetings, and perform their social and other visits, his arrangements were well contrived and his facilities liberally contributed. It is believed that more than half his time was devoted to duties of a social, religious, and humane character, in the performance of which it is not known that he was ever deterred by adverse weather.

In the delicate and responsible office of administering the discipline of the Society of Friends, Philip Price, while firm in its execution, was ever compassionate and charitable, and sincerely actuated by the desire to reclaim an erring brother, and it was only when he believed the vindication of its testimonies required it, that he concurred in the judgment of disownment from the society. In the transaction of business in its meetings, he was inclined to wait for the expression of the views of others, and if these expressed his own, he felt discharged from an obligation to repeat them. The forward he would privately counsel to observe a salutary restraint; while the diffident would receive from him encouragement in this wise,—"If we wait until we are perfect before we attempt to do good, there are few of us that can do much good. Do what appears to thee to be right for thee to do, and trust that strength will be given to go through it with consistency and with the Divine approval."

As superintendents of schools, their judicious conduct, kindness, and humanity, were conspicuously manifest In a letter recently received from Benjamin Hallowell, of Alexandria, Va., who was a teacher at West-Town, from 1821 to 1824, and a competent judge of long and yet continuing experience, he bears this testimony,—"I have always looked back to the time spent there as the most important and improving period of my life, which I attribute, mainly, to the dear Friends, Philip and Rachel Price, in immediate charge of the institution. No persons could have been more admirably qualified for such a charge. They invariably manifested towards *every member* of the large family, which, including teachers, scholars, and domestics, numbered over two hundred, the feelings of deeply concerned parents, urging to a faithful performance of individual duty, and to the maintenance of mutual kindness, confidence, and affection. In the delicate relation of umpire in cases of difficulty between teachers and scholars, the mild, deliberate, and concerned manner of the Superintendent (Philip Price), was remarkably successful. He was much opposed, from principle, to corporal punishments, and the committee who were at that time in charge of the institution, wisely adopted the regulation that previous to the teachers' resorting to this mode of correction, the case of difficulty should be laid before the Superintendent and his sanction obtained. When the men teachers all united in judgment that the conduct of a boy had been such that corporal punishment must be inflicted, they laid the case before the Superintendent. After hearing the statement of the teachers, he usually sat fifteen or twenty minutes with them in the most solemn stillness, and manifestly under an intense exercise and concern that a right judgment might prevail in the case; and I have known in repeated instances, the influence of his precious spirit so to operate upon the minds of the teachers, that, without his uttering a single word, they would unitedly propose a milder treatment; and, what it was very interesting to observe, there was not a single instance, where the milder course was adopted under these circumstances, which was not entirely satisfactory and successful in the result, verifying the expression of Scripture, 'the effectual, fervent prayer of a righteous man availeth much.'"

This narrative has so much dwelt upon the serious and solemn duties of life and religion, with which its objects were engaged, that an erroneous impression may be taken as to some of the traits of their character. It is true that a serious dignity was ever present, because they possessed a native dignity of character, and the habitual discharge of constantly recurring solemn duties naturally produced a serious thoughtfulness; but no persons were less encased by a repulsive self-righteousness, or were more attractively inviting to cheerful, happy, and innocent society. They delighted to commingle in feeling even with playful childhood, and a vein of pleasant humour kindly indulged by Philip Price towards others, and particularly the youthful, made his company always acceptable, and begot for him their confidence and affection. Thousands yet living, who have experienced the cheerful kindness, regard, and sympathy of Philip and Rachel Price, will bear their testimony to these qualities of their hearts; and travel where they might over the wide territory of our country, their descendants have ever enjoyed the happiness of finding such testimony warmly and affectionately borne to the memory of their departed parents.

Upon the subject of the ministry, our beloved mother has left some observations that it may be useful to repeat and preserve. Preaching in the will of man, and with the effort of human eloquence, she considered wholly irreconcileable with the sacredness of the service and the profession of Friends, that the Gospel ministry can only consist in the faithful delivery of the message Divinely communicated. It is, she instructs us, "an awfully responsible station to fill, to be made use of as an instrument in the hands of the Lord, and to speak to the people in His Holy name. The eye must be kept single; the blind must not lead the blind; all human importance be suppressed, nor man presume to add to or diminish the words of prophecy, lest he experience condemnation, and lose his part in the book of life. Let not the leaders of the people cause them to err, by drawing them into sects, party divisions, and controversy, wholly at variance with the spirit of true religion, which breathes peace on earth and good will to men. The temptation to arrogate consequence, and minister to the great *Myself*, ever besets poor human nature,—the king, priest, and people,—and the important 'I,' 'me,' and 'mine,' become painfully conspicuous in their emphatic and frequent use in the hearing of the unselfish and devoted worshippers of God, who ever ascribe to Him and the Saviour, the merit and glory, as they alone are the source of all that is good and perfect. These self-important teachers forget that they are no longer safe than while they obey the injunction of the Master, 'Watch and pray continually, lest you enter into temptation.' Let them not take the Lord's jewels to decorate self, and give the praise to the creature that belongs to the Creator; and let them remember the caution that even the Apostle Paul took unto himself, of the necessity of keeping the body in subjection when he preached to others, lest he should be himself a castaway. Let all who presume to speak in the name of the Lord, seriously consider the import of Christ's declarations, 'Freely you have received—freely give;' and that 'all who will come, may come, and partake of the waters of life freely, without money and without price.' I conceive there is great danger of being cast away, from the imprudent caresses of those who may feel very much attached to the favoured instruments, and who manifest their regard even unto personal flattery, of the poor frail vessel through which the pure spring of living water may flow to the people, for their refreshment and consolation. But these are only earthly vessels, subject to be injured and liable to fall, if by heeding the applause of men they become self-consequent and self-important. 'Let him who thinketh he standeth take heed lest he fall.' May the humble, self-denying followers of Christ, be encouraged to take up the cross daily, considering nothing too near or too dear to part with, so that they may obtain that crown of glory which is laid up in store for all those who love the appearance of Jesus in the heart, and yield to it in obedience."

In delineating the lives of Philip and Rachel Price, it has seemed unavoidable to speak of the faith, testimonies, and usages of the Society of Friends. In that society they "lived, moved, and had their being." Engaged in the active and practical duties of life and religion, and making communications that were chiefly oral and unpreserved, the filling up of the history of their services, character, and principles, was properly to be drawn from those of their religious society. So far as the writer has been enabled to give a correct view of these, the result cannot fail to be useful. But it is right that his own observations and reflections should be accompanied by certain cautionary remarks. He is not a member of the society, and speaks by no authority as such. He especially desires that nothing he has said may be construed as favouring either division into which Friends have unhappily separated over the other, or as casting a censure upon either. He regards that separation but with regret and sorrow; and it is irrespective of it that he has felt bound to reiterate the expression of his love and admiration of the principles, testimonies, faith, and practices of the society. He has felt great fear and delicacy in handling serious and sacred subjects, as one little authorized to touch them; while the duty of writing this Memoir of his parents, so long neglected and so likely to be wholly omitted by others, has appeared to be unmistakeable and imperative. And again, he has had the consolation of knowing that for all errors committed, no one else than himself can be held responsible, while from himself much cannot have been expected; and as no influence can be exerted further than as truth shall manifest itself to the acceptance of his readers, so will error as readily expose itself to be detected and rejected.

Since all of this volume was written except what shall now be introduced by this paragraph, a work has appeared of peculiar virulence and injustice in its charges against Friends. Such charges have been infrequent in modern times, for the world had begun to appreciate and do justice to the principles and services of the society. In the enjoyment of the happy toleration and equality of all religious persuasions under the Constitutions of these United States, where no one sect can exact tithes from those who share not in its worship; where all support to the church is a voluntary tribute, and no one can claim pre-eminence over another, the causes of irritation have so far ceased that we find all disposed kindly to co-operate in all good works, and it has become a matter of more than questionable taste and propriety for any one to attack another; for all are alike bound to respect that toleration under which each enjoys its own immunity from encroachment. There is one cause, however, yet operative to produce the recurrence of attacks upon the Society of Friends. They have ever held it to be their duty, by a mutual watchfulness and supervision, to keep their members to a consistent observance of the pure and exalted principles and conduct of their religious profession, and to disown from membership those whom patient and forbearing Christian entreaty fails to preserve from bringing a reproach upon the Gospel truth. Those who are unwilling to take up the cross and sacrifice their worldly desires and vanities, impatiently submit to the administration of the discipline, and in leaving the society, sometimes let fly their Parthian arrows envenomed by resentment. A companion of our youth, and a frequent visitor under the roof of the subjects of this Memoir, found the society, its discipline and doctrines, uncongenial to his inclinations, taste, and convictions, and employed his well remembered characteristic powers of ridicule, and his acquired biblical learning, to prove "Quakerism not Christianity;" but this eminent Presbyterian minister did not condescend to become the industrious ferreter of private vices, or the betrayer of the confidences of friendship and hospitality. His polemic work of near seven hundred pages, was sufficiently answered in a pamphlet of seventy, in "Vindication of the Society of Friends," by Enoch Lewis. This co-labourer, through life, of my parents, but yet, at near an octogenarian age, actively engaged to enlighten his fellow-citizens and serve humanity, has, in this vindication, and in all his writings and example in life, appeared to be the more valuable in his advocacy, as showing that in the same mind and bosom may reign in congenial consistency the high attainments and severe habits of thought of mathematical and abstract science, together with the belief of the inspired influences of religion, as operative on the sensibility of the heart.

The most recent attack, first above referred to, "Quakerism, or Story of my Life," is a painful exhibition, not of the indulgence of playful ridicule, or a battle upon polemical differences, but of a sad perversion of the writer's own feelings, and of her willingness to seek out foibles and delinquencies, that, so far as founded in the semblance of truth, are exceptional cases from the general rule, and evincive that she was stimulated by resentment, or prompted by an appetite that sought its own congenial food in what it fed upon. The powers of fiction that were cultivated in stolen opportunities of novel reading, in disobedience to the injunctions of her father, have been turned in abuse and disparagement of the principles and practices which that father cherished as his life; and her production involves the obvious contradictions that if the writer had not had a high appreciation of the reputation of the society, she would not have been so deeply mortified in her vanity by her disownment and deprivation of a share therein, and that without its excellent and purifying principles and practices her no doubt justly lauded father would not have had so high an estimate of them, nor have become their exponent in the pious and excellent character she describes. Did it never occur to that daughter how much she might be grieving the spirit of that father, in her unmitigated ridicule and abuse of his nearest friends and dearly cherished religious profession? It is needless, however, to attempt special refutation of her perversions and defamations, for they are apparent in the perusal of the book, and are contradicted by the history of Friends, and the every-day intercourse of all who have lived among them. Of whom can it be more fearlessly asserted that they have ever been engaged to do those things that the Saviour of men declared would obtain the blessing of the Father and the inheritance of the kingdom prepared from the foundation of the world? When have they not given to the hungered meat, to the thirsty drink, to the stranger shelter, clothed the naked, visited the sick and imprisoned? Who more sturdily fought the battle of religious freedom and political equality, and separation of Church and State, than Fox and Penn, and their associates, and gave their principles trial and example in Pennsylvania, whence they have been perpetuated in all the Constitutions of all the States of this Union? Who, but Friends, were the chief support of Wilberforce, Pitt, Fox, Clarkson, and others, when Parliament abolished the unutterable horrors of the African slave trade? Who led the way to the abolition of slavery in these States, but devoted and conscientious Friends, who yielded to the operations of the Spirit of the Almighty upon their hearts, when all the rest of mankind were blinded by self-interest, or unfaithful to the manifestations of Divine Truth? Who so humane and just towards the helpless aborigines of our continent? and who else refused to take from them by power and hold by force, natural rights, that the God of Nature had conferred upon the sons of the forest? Who but they were the pioneers in the blessed cause of temperance for ages before others were touched by the modern zeal upon that subject? Who after Howard, like Elizabeth Fry, descended into foul dungeons, and among the worse living pollutions of the prisons, for their purification and reform, sustained by the wealth and influences of brothers of kindred feelings of humanity?—yet are these the special objects of the aspersion of this perverse writer—and that even in the matter of food absolutely required by the condition of the health of a delicate and lovely woman, broken down and exhausted by her constant and devoted services for the relief of the most suffering and most neglected portions of humanity. It might reasonably have been expected that one who was sacrificing health and life for the good of others, could receive the sustenance medically advised, and required to prolong her strength yet a little longer to serve her suffering fellow-beings, without the reproach of a woman, claiming the refinement of a lady, and even a more saving faith in the religion of Jesus. But in those who respect not the memory of the good and the humane, nor yet the sanctity of the grave, what trust can we have? The Christian world will, however, believe the mark quite too high and pure to be reached by the shafts sped by private pique or malevolence. That world has already awarded to Elizabeth Fry, and to those brothers who in honouring her drafts in favour of suffering humanity honoured themselves, the homage of its praise and admiration and a world-wide renown; and when, in a holy sympathy for suffering, she gratefully thanked them with the exclamation, "What sister has such brothers as I!" and they happily replied, "What brothers have such a sister as we!" that world did them the justice to believe that this exultation of gratified feeling had its source in a pure and holy Fountain.

And who, when the world was stirred in sympathy for famished Ireland, and poured into that devoted island its stores of relief—who were so trusted and so useful in the distribution of its concentrated charity, as some of these abused Quakers, whom this self-deluded and uncharitable authoress would expect the world to believe are as a society a whited sepulchre without, and full of loathsome corruptions within? But turn we where we may, where are not the evidences of the good deeds of these Samaritan people? Everywhere they are seen to instruct the youth, clothe and feed the poor, to visit the sick and imprisoned, to teach the blind and the dumb, and to preach the Gospel, not among themselves only, but among and to all others, without money and without price. And—most blessed triumph of humanity!—they taught mankind most successfully to minister unto the most afflicted portion of humanity—to those bereft of reason—by the sure approaches of kindness and sympathy to hearts mistakenly supposed, in the prostration of a rational accountability, to be dead to all the feelings of humanity. They rescued these unfortunate beings, so often the victims of feelings that but make their sensibilities the more acute, from confinement and punishments, cruel even when inflicted for crime; struck from them fetters and shackles, fit instruments themselves to dethrone the reason and drive even sanity into madness; and brought them from dungeons into the light of day, and the presence of the glorious works of nature, and into the social intercourse and sympathy of their fellow-beings, all so soothing and restorative to the lacerated feelings, whether writhing under real or imaginary woes. So long was it before those that in ancient times were spoken of as having "a devil," were treated otherwise than if really so possessed. Some gifted medical men had suggested the beneficent idea, and partially tried the experiment of the reverse treatment; but it was in Friends' Retreat, at York, in England, and in Friends' Asylum, at Frankford, in Pennsylvania, where the happy suggestion was more effectually tried and proved for the adoption of the world. Strange, indeed, seems it now, that mankind could have expected cure to the mind from distracting exasperations, more than that the healing process could close a wound ever irritated by rude appliances and fresh inflictions. But slow has man always been to learn that the chief of human aids, to remedy all bodily or mental, moral, political or religious ailments, is to remove all causes of aggravation, thereby to permit the delicate processes of cure quietly to proceed, by the beneficently healing and restorative power that gave and preserves life, health, and mental sanity. And lastly, who follow so nearly in the footsteps of Jesus, in His example and commandments, for the preservation of good feeling and peace among men? Friends seek not political power, they claim no distinction, aspire to no earthly fame, neither is their kingdom of this world. All the favour they ask is that men should love one another, forbear to persecute, cease to injure and make war on each other, learn to do well and be happy; all the privilege they desire is to be permitted humbly to do good; and whomsoever they may aid in whatsoever cause of humanity, all that they ask is a hearty co-operation in the service, and freely and in welcome may others take all the political power and influence and fame. It sufficeth to them to enjoy the reward of an approving conscience, and humbly to hope for the final award to the good and faithful servant.

Taking leave of the Irish authoress, the narrative will proceed as it was before written, nothing deterred by her assault, from recommending the faith, the testimonies, and example of Friends, to the imitation of others. In thus endeavouring to do them some justice against a wanton attack, the language used may appear to be strong and unreserved; yet will the members of the society be the last to suppose, or to wish, that they should be represented as faultless. Some individuals will prove derelict in all religious associations; but it is in their guileless simplicity, purity of motives, and unsuspicious character, that Friends most frequently present a mark for the shafts of ridicule, or expose their motives to a sinister interpretation, by themselves unperceived and unintended. They admit the duty ever to strive to be, but do not claim to be perfect. Man's admitted imperfection and liability to err lie at the base of the structure of their church polity, which not only exacts a constant self-watchfulness, but permits and claims as a fraternal duty, watchfulness of one over another, and of all over each, wherein the counsels of the least given in an authorized concern may not be unheeded by the greatest. The constant warfare between good and evil endures through life, and as constantly and enduringly demands vigilance and the invocation of Divine aid and protection. It is the victory of righteousness over sin, that is the great and surest test of true religion, and that must be maintained unto the end. A secured perfection is unattainable by man on earth. It was under a sense of human infirmity that the mother in Israel herein commemorated, on whose pure life no cloud for a moment cast its shadow, tasked herself, even at fourscore years of age, "to double her diligence," that she might fail in no duty that could preserve her highest peace of mind, and bring to her bosom the grateful evidences of the Divine approval.

Among all the reforms and advances made by the Society of Friends, there is, perhaps, none more important and interesting to contemplate, than the improvement in the position and influence of woman. Her equality is recognised more perfectly than in any other religious community. She participates in the concerns of their meetings of business, in the executive duties of administering the discipline, in the meetings for ministers and elders, in the marriage ceremony makes only the same promise as her husband of fidelity and love, and in the service of the ministry, all are in a perfect equality before God. The result is mutually beneficial: it is humanizing to the men; it makes women more reflective and intelligent, for the faithful discharge of their responsible duties requires that they should be adequately informed, calmly deliberative, tolerant of differences of views, and capable of reconciling them to a practical result. This experience gives strength of character and mind, but does not detract from the qualities of the heart, that make women truly to be loved and respected.

It is true all other religious persuasions afford their many bright and useful examples of women who devote their lives to works of charity and humanity, and as devoutly and acceptably worship their Creator; but in none do they enjoy the same approach to an equality with men. There they are led, taught, and employed, but do not deliberate, govern, or instruct, in the higher matters of Church government and worship. It is true, too, that Quakerism plucks from the person every attractive ornament of dress, and mirth and gayety are transformed to a tranquil seriousness; yet may not the devotee of fashion and pleasure take a useful lesson from the unadorned and self-sacrificing Quakeress? The quick pulsations of pleasure rapidly exhaust the vital energies, the spirits sink, and beauty fades, beyond the power of an assumed vivacity or the skill of art to retrieve; and amidst a round of empty occupations and distrusted enjoyments, the culture of the mind and heart is neglected. Then does the advantage of a more prudent reservation of the resources of health become apparent; while the time and inclination preserved for intellectual pursuits, have made the mental improvement progressively apparent in the charms of conversation, and in the radiant expressions of the countenance. With well preserved health, with peace and happiness within, crowned with goodness and intelligence, ever advancing by constant culture, the human form and mind become the most benign and attractive in expression. The countenance lighted by intelligence, softened and harmonized by the influences of the dove-like spirit within, becomes proof against the ravages of time and of perennial beauty. The painter may exhaust the delicate skill of his exquisite art on a Madonna, or encircle with a halo of glory the sacred character of heavenly mien, but no artistic skill can successfully rival the impressive beauty of "the human face divine," when softened and illumined by the inspirations of a Divine love, and a serene intelligence and happiness.

Men who neglect the aid of women for all that is good and useful, are not true economists of the resources provided by Providence. Though it may be that other persuasions will not admit them to participate in the affairs of Church government and in the ministry, their aid and influence would be found of incalculable service in their schools, asylums, hospitals, and in various ways, in all that promotes charity, humanity, and religion, with which her feelings and nature are more congenial. Women of highest rank and cultivation, thus occupied, would derive the purest consolation and happiness, feel life to be a higher blessing, and, by their happy influence, interest and attract others to aid in their holy engagement; while we all owe it to those in humble condition to make more room for female employment in every business requiring delicacy and skill of execution without great muscular effort, guarding them against undue exposure, and from every occupation and influence that would detract from that respect and regard which a brother would wish to entertain for a sister, and a father and a husband for a daughter and wife.

Let not man, in his pride and self-sufficiency, slight the aid of woman as unimportant. She has ever aided the onward progress of Christianity and civilization, and, probably, even more than man, prevents a relapse from the vantage-ground attained. But for her constantly exerted meliorating influences, man's more rugged and ruffian nature would but become more hard, harsh, and selfish, and be but seldom adorned by the Christian graces. It is the mother that moulds the tender mind of infancy, and gives it its most abiding impress through life. She forms the character of the future mothers of the race, to repeat and perpetuate the same lessons of instruction, and also forms the character of the men who will rule the national councils and guide the destinies of mankind. Greater, it is believed, would be the loss to human welfare, if the mothers' teachings to the infant mind were lost, than if all the seminaries for the education of men were closed for ever. And as there is no influence so potent for good, so there is no sight on earth so beautiful and holy as that of the intelligent and pious mother, when at the close of the day she imbues the minds of her children with the spirit of prayer, and teaches them to recall its events for self-correction—to ask forgiveness of each other for all offences given, and of a Heavenly Father for every wrong committed. None but a mother will find the time, or will condescend to this sacred office; none can feel the same intense responsibility for these precious beings, as she that bore them; and none like her enjoy the holy bliss that kindles in her bosom, as she trains her offspring for usefulness on earth, in the confiding hope that her labours, Divinely blessed, may secure the reunion of her beloved family in Heaven. With such a hope, can so sacred a trust ever be neglected or delegated by one true to the maternal feelings? can any other than a mother fulfil the requirings of this high accountability, or finally answer in her stead the awful inquiry, should any of the precious flock be missing, "What hast thou done with the lambs committed to thy charge in the wilderness of the world?"

It were well, and it is but just, that woman should be ever impressed and encouraged by the thought that she is peculiarly, in the order of Divine Providence, designed for the accomplishment of the highest good to our race, and that man also should understand that in the strength of a towering intellect, fitted for physical, scientific, and political progress, he is less potent for good in all that constitutes true excellence of character, and gives the most assured promise of everlasting happiness.

Are these reflections seemingly a digression from the narrative? They but further illustrate the character and enforce the example of one of the best of mothers, all of whose long life was faithfully devoted to the fulfilment of these high and sacred duties. They are believed to be written, and it is humbly hoped this volume has been written, in the spirit of her last and sacredly regarded injunction, "Be obedient unto the law written in thy heart, and endeavour to draw others unto it!" It is in this faith that obstacles have been levelled in prospect, and clouds have melted into the transparency of heaven. And, again, I have been encouraged by the advice of a venerated father, to those disposed to hang back and thereby fail to do what good they might, "If we wait to be perfect before we attempt to do good, there are few that can do much good."

It is of course that the question has often recurred, and recurs with a more serious impressiveness in drawing the narrative to a close—Has it been written with a sufficient object, and with motives wholly pure? The best response afforded to an inward scrutiny and prayerful feeling has been affirmatively given. For numerous relatives and friends has the Memoir been written, and their appreciation and love for its objects will assuredly make the work acceptable to them; and should it fall into other hands, let these reflect and duly allow for the purpose of its composition. The motives that actuated in its execution, are believed in all instances to have been pure, and with an exalted aim; at all events, to have proceeded from a sense of duty, and a desire for truth and usefulness. Having this assurance, whatever censure may follow, the sacrifice will be felt to be slight, indeed, when compared with that of the natural feelings of a beloved mother, when yielding to the requisitions authoritatively made upon her.

Upon the consideration of the highest usefulness of example, can any error in this step have been committed? The history of the lives commemorated has appeared to be instructive in the best duties of the citizen, and the most sacred of the Christian; and if without the adventure and the worldly fame that arrest the attention and dazzle the fancy, it will shed a mild and beneficent light, usefully to guide the humble, the industrious, and the devoted, who would serve their fellow-beings and walk acceptably in the sight of their Maker. It will excite no eccentric ambition to leave the quiet and peaceful walks of private life, and, affording examples within the reach of imitation by all, will become the more extensively useful. Mankind, as they become more enlightened and humanized, sicken at the shedding of human blood, and relish less the details of the horrors of war. The heroes of humanity, and the victories of peace, become more attractive and admired. By the test that goodness is to be preferred to greatness, the good most deserve to be held in remembrance, and upheld as examples. Since "he that is slow to anger, is better than the mighty, and he that ruleth his spirit, than he that taketh a city," how much better then those who have not only all their lives submitted to the restraining power of religion, but have by active service devoted those lives to the good of their fellow-beings!

Those who shall have attentively followed the writer through this narrative, cannot have failed to make the reflection that from a point of small beginning, the subjects of this Memoir underwent a most useful mental culture and religious improvement. This growth is easily explained: They were faithful to the little furnished, and became rulers over more. Their school instruction consisted of the rudiments of an English education, imperfectly obtained in country schools, at the period of the revolution. But their minds were early brought under an exercise of feeling that necessarily induced a further and higher culture. Religion comes with its strongest power upon those minds who believe their impressions to be the inspeaking word of the Almighty to His dependent children. Under its influence a scrutiny commences upon the conduct, affections, and thoughts, more rigid and unsparing than the Socratic cross-questioning of feelings and motives; and to prove faithful to a trust of the most sacred obligation, the duty of self-watchfulness, and of a conduct conformed to the manifestations received, becomes incessant and imperative. Under this high sanction, they felt themselves charged to seek their souls' salvation, and commissioned to turn the minds of others to the only true source of their redemption. Fidelity to this trust was more to them than life or death. It was a requisition of a like resistless obligation to that which caused their religious ancestors to endure persecutions unto imprisonment and death; and that it was which required a modest, delicate, and retiring woman to overcome her great natural reluctance, and to stand up before the assemblies of the people, and to travel abroad to preach the Gospel. No other incentive could be so strong upon the human mind, to seek and to hold fast all that was good for instruction and spiritual profit, and this higher cultivation of the mind, and process of purifying the human affections, necessarily increased the intelligence, and gave elevation to the thoughts of those undergoing this authoritative teaching. The author of Elia tells his readers—lovers of literature—to "Get the writings of John Woolman by heart; and love the early Quakers." The subjects of this Memoir read for something more than the indulgence of a literary taste. They read to establish their faith—to strengthen their resolution in a devoted service—to "be perfect and thoroughly furnished unto good works." They read with deepest sympathy and undoubting faith, the Holy Scriptures, the writings and histories of early Friends, many of them good scholars; and they heard the preaching and conversations of contemporaries, at a period when many eminent men and women adorned the ranks of their society. It was a training to enlarge the mind and improve the heart; to form serious, reflective, and earnest character, and to blend in it the firmest resolution, with the mildest disposition, and a sympathy for others' woe. The command was ever before them, "Be ye perfect, even as your Father which is in Heaven is perfect," and ever watchfully striving for purification and refinement, they attained to a higher excellence than practicable under any other teaching. They lived in the beauty of holiness, and the brightness of the world they beheld before them illumined that below, and made their character here reflective of the stainless purity of the life to come.

The review of these pages happily presents nothing of a controversial character; and nothing of the kind, as connected with the characters commemorated, has been suppressed. On the sure foundation they started in life, these faithful Friends continued unto the end. It was that on which the Society of Friends rose distinctively in the beginning, whose doctrine and testimonies the world then resented, but become more enlightened, has been more willing to acknowledge to be generally truthful and righteous. The lives here portrayed, abiding in the love that distinguished their religious ancestry, and in the light and life of the Gospel, as made manifest by the Holy Scriptures, and the revealings of Divine truth upon the souls of men, were in all of life consistent exponents of the true Quaker character. With them the precious seed fell neither upon stony ground, nor was it choked by thorns. The first public appearance of one, was with the declaration, that "God is a spirit, and they that worship Him aright must worship Him in spirit and in truth, for it is such *He seeketh* to worship Him," and among the last, "*To know* Thee, the only True God, and Jesus Christ whom *Thou hast sent*, this is life eternal;" and in the lives of both, all was consistent with these declarations. Their religion was a religion in its highest power—a vital principle, inwardly active, and productive of a living faith and love, worship and works, prayer and praise; and in the same faith and love they lived, so they died, in the confident hope of a happy and glorious immortality.

In gathering these scattered fragments, the writer has derived instruction which he sincerely hopes may be experienced by others. He has felt the task to be a small reparation for the neglect of former opportunities, when the best of parents spoke in living tones, in the faith that even neglected counsels might return as bread cast upon the waters, after many days. So have they been felt to return to him in this labour of love and gratitude, and so may they return as the bread of life to others, and float down the stream of time to successive generations of descendants. In meditating upon their sweet and peaceful memory, his sorrow for their loss has been soothed by their precious words of hope, and his aspirations encouraged by their beneficent example. In these renewed associations and tender recollections, he has felt that "there is a joy in grief, when peace dwells in the breast of the sad"—a "pleasant joy of grief, like the shower of spring, when it softens the branch of the oak, and the young leaf rears its head;" and his earnest prayer is, that their words and example may pass on, alike refreshingly, to remoter generations, nourishing into spiritual life and the beauty of holiness, and their course be made freshly visible by beneficent effects, "as willows by the watercourses."

And I thank Thee, my Heavenly Father, that Thou hast permitted me to accomplish this filial duty; and hast caused the touch of the dry and mouldering relics of thy departed servants to impart a renovated life. In the performance of the service, Thou hast given increase of strength, shed upon the wakeful hours of night an unwonted light, and mingled in the busy day its purest joy. Thou hast awakened long slumbering emotions of the heart, whispered to the ear the sweet tones familiar to youthful days, as in distant echoes from my native hills, and led me again over their green pastures as one of the flock that knoweth the voice of the True Shepherd; and again have I listened to the pathetic tones of a devoted Mother's Gospel ministry, and a dedicated Father's counsels of wisdom. May all their descendants, in the retrospection now afforded, aided by Thy Holy Spirit, enjoy the like happy experience. May the sweet memories of the distant past, thus influenced, cause again and often to flow in their breasts the pure fountain of living waters, leaving none to thirst again; and with the baptism of joyous tears may Thy heavenly spirit approvingly descend upon them. Take from every error here committed the power to harm; cure every wound here inflicted by the instillations of Thy healing balm; and commission these leaves to take their flight only for good. May these gathered thoughts, as winged seeds borne upon the breeze, fall upon goodly soil, and, nourished by Heavenly dews, spring into life, in their blossom yielding a grateful fragrance unto Thee, and in their fruit righteousness and eternal life.

ELI K. PRICE.

INDEX.

THE END.

www.ingramcontent.com/pod-product-compliance
Lightning Source LLC
LaVergne TN
LVHW011019110820
845150LV00006B/1478
9781425516369